AFRICAN-AMERICAN SPIRITUALITY, THOUGHT & CULTURE

AFRICAN-AMERICAN SPIRITUALITY, THOUGHT & CULTURE

DR. PHYLLIS BAKER

iUniverse, Inc.
New York Lincoln Shanghai

AFRICAN-AMERICAN SPIRITUALITY, THOUGHT & CULTURE

iUniverse books may be ordered through booksellers or by contacting:

iUniverse
2021 Pine Lake Road, Suite 100
Lincoln, NE 68512
www.iuniverse.com
1-800-Authors (1-800-288-4677)

ISBN: 978-0-595-44231-7 (pbk)
ISBN: 978-0-595-88562-6 (ebk)

Printed in the United States of America

Contents

ACKNOWLEDGEMENTS

I would like to acknowledge and honor the following persons who helped to make this work possible and who have contributed so much to my development. My deepest respect and gratitude to my parents Abner & Zenovious Sermons-Stripling. I would like to thank Dr. Carole Boyce-Davies who offered helpful editorial comments and suggestions on short notice. I would like to honor Dr. Delridge Hunter and Babaca M' Bow, for their friendship, inspiration, encouragement and scholarly advise to complete this work. I can never thank pastor and teacher Reverend Dr. Mary Tumpkin enough, who I have learned so much from over the years. I give appreciation to my children's father, Robert Baker, for his help and support; to my sons B.J. and Brian who are the light of my life. To my spiritual advisors Mattie Rolle, and Queen Esther Hopkins, I thank you for your guidance. My Department Chairperson, German Munoz, for he makes teaching a pleasure, and gave me my first opportunity to become published. Many thanks to my editors Ruby Moaney, Tawnicia Ferguson-Rolle, and Dr. Hunter for their editorial recommendations and assistance. To Norma, Paulette, Loretta, Greer, Patricia, Jahmal Westmoreland-EL, Dr. Paul George, the Sojourner Book Club, and all of my family, friends, students, and to my entire academic family at Florida International University and Miami Dade College, thank you.

INTRODUCTION

This book is an attempt to make sense to myself; and to help other people understand themselves. Additionally, this works seeks to resurrect the souls of the ancestors, so we may draw from their knowledge, their power and their strength. It is to assist in putting our lives in perspective and provide a context that is meaningful and holistic. This work is for other ethnic and cultural groups as well, in an effort for them to gain some clarity and appreciation for the spiritual and cultural heritage of African Americans. In truth, there are some universal truths and principles that transcend culture. Perhaps this work can bring to light an understanding of how very fascinating human beings really are, particularly when viewed from a historical, cultural and spiritual context.

This work supports the position that spirituality and relationships (Love) kept black people from losing their minds. Psychologists tell us that African Americans and other minorities in general, have more stress than the larger population (Duffy).

Historically, African-Americans have been psychologically and physically devastated. How did they survive a Middle Passage (the voyage on slave ships across the Atlantic Ocean) that was so serious and cruel? Many African people on those ships not only were terrified, but endured malnutrition, dehydration; cramped and inhuman traveling conditions, measles, diarrhea, small pox and many were killed before arriving to these shores. Certainly, these were not "the love boats". There is an account that indicated that 240 Africans died on one ship from disease (Thornton).

Africans had to face the psychological shock of being separated from their children, mates, and other family members and friends, their entire worlds were turned upside down. One observer noted "African People are full of sadness and depression" It is amazing that a group that has faced so much has been able to survive, and in many cases thrive. Some Africans coming to this country thought that their blood would be used to make flags like the ones on the slave ships. Others were taught to believe that their bodies would be used to make gun power and oil. This is the type to Psychological trauma Africans had to endure (Thornton).

Plantation life was no picnic either, work was hard and dangerous, and many died from accidents and deplorable working conditions. Rapes, beatings and hard work were a part of daily life. Then the long road of Jim Crow laws and injustice, and all of the humiliation, disrespect, and suffering, that goes with it. Yet they are still here. Why? And How? Many believe it was largely based on the African Spiritual Practices that survived and were retained here in the United States. This book will discuss some of those practices and beliefs.

I contend that many African-Americans are still in recovery, and healing is still occurring. This work gives us an account and perspective of some of the tools used by African-Americans to this point in history and can help move them into the future. This book is an attempt to add to the cultural discourse and provide spiritual practices that can continue to make African-Americans strong and masterful.

In this book you will be asked to engage in three (3) Exercises: Maintain a Prayer Journal, Dream Journal and a Music Journal.

"WE MUST REMEMBER THE SOULS OF BLACK FOLK"

1

AFRICANIZED CHRISTIANITY

Deep within the African American Community are rich and mystical spiritual traditions. These traditions combine traditional African religious practices with Christian religious practices, and is referred to here as Africanized Christianity. These concepts of synchronism of thoughts and beliefs have been largely unexplored by Black Scholars and other segments of the population, for its roots lie largely within the Black Church Experience.

African-Americans are descendents of spiritual zealots whose entire existence and survival were based on the interaction of spiritual and mystical forces. Theses forces are believed to be responsible for prosperity and poverty, sickness and health, freedom and bondage and every other conceivable aspect of life. Traditional African Religions are largely based on sacrifice; African American religions are based on sacrifice as well, the "sacrifice of praise." To witness an African American religious service generally means the witness of a highly interactive, totally engaging, highly emotional, spirit filled and charged service. These religious experiences tend to embrace the notion of "Making a Joyful Noise". Sound, movement, and faith are the major components that set these forces into motion. The sounds of music and drums, the sounds of the "Preacher Man or Woman" The sounds of the "Prayer Warriors", the sounds of the congregations responding, and participating in the collective energy, or worship experience, provides for an awe inspiring and fascinating experience. The audience is constantly exhorted to stand, wave them hands, (put those hands in the air) clap and "say amen." It is a requirement to do something. Somewhere within the African-American Soul and or Culture is the need to physically express, move, sing, shout or jump, thereby implying an action oriented spirituality. All are encouraged to join in, for it is a community process and community affair. The scripture that says, "Where two or three are gather in my name ..." (Mathew 18:20) has special significance for African-Americans. It is believed that 'this way' is pleasing to God, and one's 'reasonable service' and responsibility.

This highly participatory and energetic spiritual manifestation is difficult to quantify, in that many in the tradition are bred from birth into this type of worship experience. This intensity is powerful and is directly related to the Black cultural ethos and speaks to the Black psyche that has been acquired, shared, guarded, and passed on to future generations. Most, if not all, African-Americans have attended one of these services, or have friends or relatives that do. These traditions and practices have been further preserved within the family by the "praying parent" who on every occasion is admonishing their children to "Have Faith," "God will make a way" "Put God first in your life", "Don't forget to pray!", and "Go to church, baby." This is demonstrated publicly at awards and celebration events and programs when African-Americans are the recipients. For many of them the first thing that comes out of their mouth is "I WANT TO THANK GOD." Even those in highly secular professions generally acknowledge God as "Their Source." African-Americans have an abiding belief in the "Spirit World" as a result; many believe that they in some significant way are intimately joined and connected to a magnificent mystical source. Many in the culture hold that they are conversant with this spiritual realm, and interact with this realm at will through the avenues of worship, dreams, trance, visual projections, and faith.

African American Religious traditions uphold and support a spiritual consciousness that is likened to a sort of "six sense" or "second nature". African-Americans being the benefactors of this belief system (yet spirit is accessible to all) are recipients and are deeply cognizant of their "power source". As a result, many have sustained and strengthened their cultural practices and beliefs over many millennia. Imagine if these traditions were more understood, harnessed and directed? This knowledge in addition to the examination of its ancient African roots would allow for greater manifestations. The African American Mysteries and knowledge are certainly worth further investigation. The African American Soul (I speak in general terms) has been grounded and molded out of struggle, faith, and a deep belief God. Over the years, great needs have called for and tested these beliefs and practices. They have proven to be a source of comfort and great power.

The question is what are the historical and cultural retentions and elements that have informed the beliefs and practices of African-American People? These traditions are mixed and mingled with African Traditional Religious practices, along with Christianity and as quiet as it is kept, occasionally, influenced by The Nation of Islam. For some African-Americans have also been touched by the work and inspired by Elijah Muhammad and his messengers. His call for Black self-sufficiency and self-empowerment, a wholesome diet, and other philosophies have also played a role in the development of African American Spiritual Consciousness. This relationship however will be saved for future and further analysis. For this work will examine the ways in which African-Americans have combined traditional African practices with Christianity.

Non-Black scholars have tried to explain this phenomenon; however, this is a difficult task because if there is no personal experience, there is a very limited context for this type of analysis. As a result, African religious practices are described disrespectfully and inadequately. Many Black scholars share a collective shame or embarrassment about what has been described as primitive practices. Still others believe it may be perceived as black magic, which, because it immediately denotes a negative connotation, should be kept hidden. Only those who are a part of the experience know the reality.

This shame or embarrassment is costly. A closer scrutiny of this knowledge may serve as a great methodology for healing and spiritual empowerment. Only then can it be determined whether this is a source of historical, cultural, and spiritual information. A thorough study can ascertain whether this is a legacy to be shared with black children, the academy, and other aspects of the community.

The "Out of Africa" theory is a prevalent theory in anthropology today. This theory holds that Africa is the birthplace of human kind and human culture. If this is true, it is only logical to deduct that Africa embodies ancient spiritual or shamanist knowledge, as well (Ember 110*). The Way of the Shaman* states the following:

> Shamanism represents the most widespread and ancient methodological system of mind, body, and healing known to humanity.

> Archaeological and ethnological evidence suggest that shamanic methods are at least twenty or thirty thousand years old. Quite possibly, the methods have much greater antiquity for, after all, primates that could be called human have been on the planet for more than two or three million years (Harner 40).

Harner defines a shaman as "a man or woman who enters an altered state of consciousness, at will, to contact and utilize an ordinarily hidden reality in order to acquire knowledge, power, and to help other persons."

Today, shamanic knowledge survives primarily among people who, until recently, had primitive (ancient) cultures. This knowledge that they preserve was acquired over hundreds of human generations, in situations of life and death. The ancestors of these peoples painstakingly learned and used this knowledge in their efforts to maintain health and strength to cope with serious illness, and to deal with the threat and trauma of death. These custodians of the ancient methods are very important to mankind, for almost none of their cultures left written records. Thus, it is only from their remaining living representatives that we can learn the shamanic principles (Harner 40). Africans on the continent and in the Diaspora are examples of this living representation. It is the study and observation of African retentions (and other ancient cultures) that enables researchers to dig to the core of deep and authentic spiritual truths.

John Thornton in his book *Africa and Africans in the Making of the Atlantic World, 1400-1800*, writes,

> As with the other elements of culture, religion responded both to its internal dynamic and to the new dynamic created by culture contact and physical transfer. The result was the emergence of a new Afro-Atlantic religion that was often identified as Christian, especially in the New World, but was a type of Christianity that could satisfy both African and European understanding of religion (Thornton 235).

The merging of religions required much more that the blending of the belief systems of both religions. It required a re-evaluation of the ideas, concepts, and sources of knowledge of both religions in order to find common ground. The major commonalities were, first of all, a belief in religion, and secondly, that ideas and images were received or revealed from non-worldly beings in one form or another. The synchronisms occurred largely in the interpretation and revelation of that spirit world in which both religious systems believed (Thornton 235-236).

These similarities assisted in the blending and merging of the African and European cosmologies and facilitated the development of an Africanized Christianity. It was, however, an imperfect fit in that in Christian thought the revelation is fixed and in African thought there is a continuous stream of revelations being given to the faithful. Thornton writes:

> African revelations of the sixteenth and seventeenth centuries can be divided into several categories. Augury and divination involve the study of events to determine other-worldly intentions. Dream interpretation relies on the notion that the other world can sometimes communicate through the unconscious mind. More dramatic revelations came in the form of visions or hearing voices, usually only by people with special gifts. Perhaps the most dramatic form or revelation was given through the spirit medium or possessed object, in which an otherworldly entity took over a human, animal, or material object and spoke through it (Thornton 239).

African-American mysticism in a church context is not expressed as such. Many people are not even aware of the link it has to ancient African heritage. In particular, the Pentecostal experience in the United States adapted and incorporated an enormous amount of Africanisms and spiritual practices of the African ancestors. Speaking in tongues, shouting, dancing in the spirit, being slain in the spirit, spirit possessions, visions, and prophecies, were used as sources to channel and interact with spiritual forces in Africa.

African-Americans tend to have a deep interest in and respect for the spirit world and spiritualisms. Even in hip-hop culture, Sunday radio programs set aside time for gospel music. This reverence was passed on to African-Americans from Africa, when their ancestors crossed the Atlantic over four hundred years ago. These beliefs and practices came with them as a way to honor the spirit world.

Many cultural and religious groups are returning to their roots to reclaim their spiritual heritage. The Jewish tradition of Kabala, also called magic, is being reborn in the lives of many Jews and non-Jews as well. The Islamic tradition of Sufism is resurfacing and is becoming increasingly popular in some circles. The Gnostic traditions of Judaism and Christianity are being studied in university circles. African-Americans and other cultural groups must learn to appreciate their mystical traditions and sacred sciences.

To understand, appreciate and activate African-American mysticism, it is important to examine its ancient shamanic roots. Before religion became religion it was called shamanism. A shaman is a person who has the ability to go into other worlds and bring back information.

At the heart of traditional African thought is a belief in the reality of a superhuman agency. Across the African continent, people experience reality as greater than the empirical aspects of nature and society. In African religions, along with tangible realities there exist a variety of gods, goddesses, and impersonal spirits and forces. Furthermore, most traditional African religions assert that three domains—the social world (human beings), the natural world, and the supernatural world—are mutually dependent. Instead of autonomous realities, these domains exist in an ordered system of relationships. Far from being chaotic, these domains of reality and the mutually defining relationships between them constitute a religious cosmos (Carter 179).

The African-American mystical ethos also views this world and all of its aspects as part and parcel of a spirit driven domain. People and all aspects of human affairs are regulated and influenced by the spirit world. This preoccupation with the superhuman agency became a prime cause of deep metaphysical beliefs and expressions.

The structure of the domains of existence in Africa varies by ethnic group. Based on their cultural structure and analysis, group members make decisions based on how they should behave, define themselves, and structure their communities (Carter 179).

These beliefs and various terms of engagement uphold the notion that the High God is extremely powerful, highly potent, and able to affect the lives of people. This power is fully accessible and can become physically expressible. These very strong beliefs set the stage for a highly developed faith faculty that is central and key to any powerful mystical tradition. For African-Americans, these beliefs blended and synchronized with Christian ideology; what results is a form of Christianity, drawing heavily on African cosmology and African expressions.

The merging of religions requires something more than simply mixing form and ideas from one religion with those of another. It requires a reevaluation of the basic concepts and sources of knowledge of both religions in order to find common ground. Religion as it was experienced in the sixteenth and seventeenth centuries was not simply an intellectual conception made up by people and subject to reconsideration and debate; rather, the ideas and the images were received or revealed from non worldly beings in one form or another, and the human role was simply to interpret these revelations and act accordingly. Thus, religious philosophy was not the creation of religion; revelations were. Religious philosophy simply interpreted them (Thornton 235-236).

For many African ethnic groups, religious ritual became a major part of life. Appeasing and satisfying spirits who had different preferences in terms of food, drink, color, and sacred activity took up a great part of the day. This level of devotion to a spiritual discipline made for a perfect fit with Christian doctrine, which required dedication, devotion, worship, and service. Again, the notion of sacrifice to God is what Black people knew already, and did very well. Additionally, Blacks where able to make contact with this superhuman agency utilizing spiritual disciplines. The oral tradition was a primary way of gaining access to the spirit world. In the words of writer Zora Neale Hurston, "the Negro is the lord of sound." African Americans, using the oral traditions of singing, praying, preaching, drumming, and music making, are allowed to enter this realm. These sounds, which are activated by a pure (sanctified) heart, served as a trigger to spirit possessions.

This analysis would be incomplete without some mention of the importance of the ancestors, who are vital to any analysis of African and African–American Thought. In the article "African Religion," J. Carter writes:

> Along with the High Gods and lesser deities, most African religions recognize another class of superhuman agency: ancestors. While not every African group actively worships ancestors, most assume recently dead family members can continue to influence their descendants. These beings are considered the "living dead." Ordinarily, they are individuals whose socially admirable qualities like moral integrity, longevity, and wealth allow them to retain a degree of prominence after death. In this way, surviving family members, by remembering the name, character, and exploits of their ancestor, likewise keeps alive certain social relationships, rights and responsibilities (Carter 181).

In the African-American church experience, ancestors are reverenced in a number of ways. In some churches they are remembered by having their pictures in the edifice. Their names are called during special occasions and at special events like Founder's Day and special gravesite visits. Their names are displayed on windows, pews, and other places in the church. On special days like Mother's Day and Father's Day it is customary to wear a red rose if one's parents are alive and a white flower if the parent is deceased (an ancestor). When believers accept the role of parenthood and passing on the family name, respect is also given to ancestors. The desire to make family members proud by performing a certain duty or task is another apparent of honoring ancestors. As an example of its importance in the Diaspora, Ancestor's Day is an official holiday in Haiti. In this manner, Haitians, like others of the Diaspora, pay homage to the "old souls." This is a long standing practice in many parts of Africa, particularly West Africa, where African Americans share a strong cultural link. Another traditional way of honoring and remembering the elders and ancestors is in the naming process. Many African-Americans named their children after senior or departed family members. This was another visible and tangible way to pay homage and respect to them.

Some African-Americans believe it is the ancestor that comes to you when you die to rejoin you and guide you through the transition from life to death. There have been many accounts in near death experiences where the spirit guide was a beloved departed relative. These beliefs and experiences are very much alive in the African-American experience.

There is an African Proverb that states, "Old folks are almost ghost." This expresses the importance of the elders or senior members of the community. In some African societies, younger members are required to have permission from the oldest member in the group before addressing the congregation. In the African–American church culture this level of homage is demonstrated in the roles of the Church Mother, Mothers Board, Deacon Boards, and the various "Elder Boards." The senior members take very active roles in the leadership, worship services, and ceremonies of the church.

Spirit Possessions

In many Western African societies and other parts of the African Diaspora, there exist the "possessions phenomena." For many, this is the ultimate spiritual experience, or certainly an ultimate goal. The spirit possession is one of the most spectacular and powerful expressions of traditional African spirituality. It is an awe-inspiring moment where the supernatural interacts with the human form. Spirit Possessions in the African American communities generally occur within the Black church experience, particularly in Pentecostal or Full Gospel churches. They are interpreted as a sign that the "Holy Spirit" or "Holy Ghost" is in the presence of the individual or congregation.

A spirit possession can be compared to an out of body experience. The worshiper's personality temporarily leaves the body or is subdued to be occupied by another or higher entity. He or she may, during this possession, shake, scream, tremble, run, dance, speak in tongues, or exhibit a combination of these behaviors. Some devotees experiencing spirit possession are believed to be endowed with supernatural abilities to heal and give prophecies or other warnings. Others may pass out in the spirit, leaving them in a partially unconscious state. However it manifests, spirit possession is interpreted as the supreme union with the spirit. It fulfills a very special need for a deep and intimate relationship or merging with the spiritual realm. Possession is a very intense experience, in some cases appearing contagious as it moves from one worshiper to another. Zora Neale Hurston writes:

> There can be little doubt that shouting is a survival of the African "possession" by the gods. In Africa it is sacred to the priesthood or a Colytes; in America it has become generalized. The implication is the same, however. It is a sign of special favor from the spirit that it chooses to drive out the individual consciousness temporarily and use the body for its expression (Hurston 91).

Drumming, music, song, and a powerful message can facilitate spirit possessions. They serve as conduits to alternate states of consciousness. Drumming and music significantly affect the brain through the central nervous system. The high and low frequencies allow for energy to be transmitted to the brain. Rhythmic and repetitive sounds affect the electrical activity of the brain by activating the theta and beta levels. Spirit possessions can be amplified and intensified by accompanying "power words (Harner)."

Spirit possessions are believed to be useful in healing sessions. An African woman explains:

> ... an occasional healer can [activate N/um (the powerful healing force)] through solo singing or instrumental playing ... the usual way of activating N/um is through the medicinal curing ceremony; or trance dance around the fire, sometimes for hours. The music, the strenuous dancing, the smoke, the heat of the fire, and the healer's intense concentration causes their N/um to heat up. When it comes to a boil, trance is achieved (Stostak 259-260).

Prayer Meeting & Devotional Services

Prayer meetings and devotional services are essential elements of the African American mystical/church experience. They are the heart and soul of the renewal and maintenance process, keeping worshipers in touch with the divine and allowing for fellowship and communion with other "sisters and brothers in the Lord." These contacts are useful tools for sharpening the spiritual senses.

Prayer meetings and devotional services are lead by Prayer Warriors, as they are termed in the Pentecostal Churches. These are usually "seasoned saints" with a high degree of church or spiritual credibility. Most are good and strong singers, very spiritually grounded, well with words, inspirational, and generally have very strong personalities. These warriors are highly skilled communicators with a depth of knowledge and insight in the moving of the spirit.

The prayers, songs, and praise take the worshipers to a deeper level. Each round goes higher and higher until the saints get caught up in a rapture of spiritual ecstasy. If this is assisted by skilled musicians, the service is enriched and the spiritual experience is heightened. Music and spirituality are and have always been the African's major power source. African people are keenly perceptive and receptive of energy. They passed down through the ages an understanding of how to recognize, harness, and utilize spiritual or psychic power. These forces have preserved and electrified African people across time and space. They have in many ways been the secret to their success and stamina over the ages.

In many Baptist Churches, it is a deacon who leads the congregation into song and prayer. The deacon usually lines out a hymn, and the worshipers follow him in the song he selects. This is an example of the "Call and Response" methodology used in Africa. After the song, the selected deacons then lead the church members into prayer. This pattern continues until this part of the service is completed. In some churches, there is a time allotted in the devotional service for testimonials. This is open to all present to share with the church what God has done for them that week, or what challenges they have overcome. This part of the service is used to edify the body of God. It helps to build the faith of the listener, by reminding them of all that God can do and has done in their lives. It also makes the audience aware of what is going on with the members, who can then receive the support they need.

Fasting

Fasting is another spiritual discipline utilized in the full gospel or Pentecostal Black churches. The saints are quick to tell you that "great things happen when you fast and pray," which they also refer to as "turning your plate down." When the pastor or another church leader calls a fast, the members respond according to their individual needs. Some people fast until 12:00 noon; others fast until 6:00 pm. For really strong needs, some members may fast for three days and three nights. During fasting periods, participants generally give up sex and unnecessary "worldly" activities in addition to food.

Fasting is one of the most powerful spiritual disciplines. When one makes the sacrifice of not eating and not giving in to the pleasures of the flesh, something amazing happens. The focus is turned toward the spiritual aspects of life: "Where attention goes, energy flows." This attunement activates the faith and will faculties to such an extent that things move and happen for your benefit. "As in the inner, so in the outer."

All of the spiritual laws are activated on your behalf: The Law of Desire, The Law of Giving, the Law of Intentionality, and The Law of Synchronicity are a few. Many of these spiritual laws are discussed in the "Kyballion," an Ancient Egyptian Text.

Fasting can cause an elevated shift in consciousness. During a fasting period it is not uncommon for some people to have out of body experiences; many are caught up between various dimensions of space and time. They meet and commune with divine spirits; they experience profound visions and dreams. Fasting is serious business.

When fasting is coupled with prayer, something great is going to happen.

Fasting also provides side health benefits for the African-American mystic. It allows the digestive system to rest, and it causes impurities and toxins to leave the body. Additionally, it is a wonderful tool for weight control.

The Preacher

The preacher is a combination of a griot (story teller) and a priest, and is usually the most outstanding spiritual figure in the group. This person is powerful in his or her oratorical abilities. He or she is a great translator and interpreter of spiritual truths. The preacher has insight, knowledge, and in some cases, other spiritual gifts, i.e. healing, singing, or discernment. The preacher is highly inspirational, charismatic, and prolific. The Black preacher usually has some notable status in the community, is highly anointed (spiritually gifted), and has the uncanny ability to cause a tremendous move in people.

The preacher in the Black church tends to use a similar call and response method to the ones used in various African ethnic groups. The Black church has been the most viable and important social institution outside the family. It has been at the forefront for civil rights and the enhancement of education and social uplift. The best of the best in terms of community and civic leadership has come from the pulpit. The black preacher serves as counselor, consoler, therapist, healer, and fortuneteller and prophet. There is a great deal of African American mysticism that resides in the office of pastor/preacher. One of the most mystical expressions of the office of the Black preacher is the "call" into the ministry. Sometimes this happens in a dream, sometimes in a vision, and sometimes it comes as a prophecy. However it comes, the call is always described as a profound experience.

Conclusion

It can be concluded, if a culture has no historical foundation, it has no traceable legacy. With this thought in mind, it is important to be vigilant, steadfast, and unmovable in preserving the knowledge of Africa. It is important to recall and remember.

Spirituality for African-Americans has been the bridge over troubled waters, the lifeblood of a strong and brilliant people. When a group celebrates their religion, they celebrate their heritage and culture. Culture is the sum total of the way people think, believe, create, and perceive the world. Culture is material and non-material. Religion is the non-material culture of African peoples. It is extremely vital that people understand their cultural ethos in order to understand themselves. Without this analysis, a person becomes disconnected, weak, unbalanced, and deeply neurotic. The methodologies and practices discussed in this work have assisted African-American people to progress through the challenges of slavery and segregation. Certainly, the methods are worthy of attention, respect, and reflection. It is imperative that one should not forget the power of their abiding faith and beliefs.

In remembering, a number of benefits can be derived:

1. A more enriched spiritual life.

2. A greater appreciation of human existence.

3. Cultivation of inner strength and guidance.

4. Power to help, heal, and transform.

5. Clarity and understanding of universal order.

6. Harmony and personal control.

7. Greater cultural and spiritual knowledge.

8. Enhanced psychological integration.

9. Increased understanding of the universality of humankind.

10. Enhanced multicultural literacy.

"REMEMBERING ZORA ..."

2

ZORA NEALE HURSTON

The acclaimed anthropologist of Black popular culture, writer, folklorist, and consultant to the Born in Slavery Series, containing conversations with "ex-slaves," playwright, and graduate of Barnard College, Zora Hurston uniquely and significantly contributed to understanding Black Life and Culture. She accomplished this by presenting the research and folklore she collected to an open audience for popular consumption. What made Hurston works profound was how they expressed the language and culture of everyday people. Her insistence on expressing the language, spirit and life of Black popular culture informs us that the "Black Soul Lives." Hurston's expertise on Black culture allowed her to expose the principles and ingredients of this culture.

Zora Neale Hurston was born in Eatonville, Florida on January 7, 1891. This is located in Central Florida. Her father, John Hurston, served as mayor for three terms in Eatonville. This was a Black community that was incorporated as a town. Being a Black town made it unique in that the people acted as any incorporated entity operates, they made laws, participated in commerce, and enjoyed a social life that was vibrant, filled with energy and reflected how black popular culture functioned during that period that Zora Hurston was growing up.

Hurston's mother, referred to as the "smartest" and "prettiest" woman in Eatonville, was intent on helping her children realize their greatness. She exalted them to strive to reach the top. She recognized Zora's intellect, spark, fortitude, and strong temperament and ability to process things around her, unlike anyone else her age. She appeared older than she was because of her intuitive understanding of Eatonville and Black people. Her knowledge of her community prepared Professor Hurston to study the Black experience in the United States, the Caribbean Islands and Central America. Her studies debunked the stereotypes perpetuated about Black people during the time she grew up. In other words, the mother of

Zora discovered during her early age, that she was unique and special. Never did she attempt to "put out that fire." Zora, being one of eight children, added to her understanding of family life, Black culture and her relationship to these important elements of Black life.

At a young age Hurston wanted to be independent. She became a lady's maid for a theatrical company. Finding that unrewarding she was intent on attending college. She attended Morgan Academy, (now Morgan State University, in Baltimore, Maryland) where she met Professor Holmes. It was Professor Holmes who introduced Ms Hurston to the language of her people. He inspired her by exposing her to the world and magic of letters. It was in poetry that she found the key to life. She later attended Howard University, for a short time, where her writings won her acknowledgement and a scholarship to Barnard College/Columbia University in Morningside Heights, New York. She graduated Barnard College in 1929.

Her talent took her into the inner circle of the Harlem Renaissance, where she was met with mixed feelings. Sometimes it was her personality, brashness, and willingness to criticize the shame in which many of her contempories felt about Black popular culture. She decided not to play the game of following the Jones, she was not embarrassed about Black cultural forms and norms, and she was unwilling to compromise what she knew to be factual information about Black popular culture. She was adamant about the value of the culture of Black people in its current form. Her raw style and "tell it like it is" presentation was not always accepted as counteracting the attacks on Black popular culture and therefore her scholarship was attacked as "airing dirty linen." As a result some ostracized her.

Hurston's work was no doubt also influenced by a father who was not only a politician but also a preacher. While this is not an uncommon combination in the African American Culture, Hurston used it to her benefit, as she closely observed the inter-workings of Black religion as a child and young adult. Later, she conducted extensive research on African American folklore and religion. She knew and wrote about Black religious life intimately. For her, Black religion was up close and personal. It was not only an academic interest but also a family and community matter. In the book entitled the Sanctified Church, Huston's vast knowledge and experiences of Black religious life are revealed and documented. In it she outlines and discusses the way Black people express their Christianity in the Sanctified Churches, which was for her an Africanized style worship experience. Hurston was also of the opinion that African Americans draw on their African cosmology and utilize the spirit world in a most far-reaching manner. Hurston described these services as extremely intense and highly spirit driven.

She chronicles the spiritual possessions, which she described as the most profound and amazing spiritual phenomena. It is a super forceful experience that takes over temporarily, the donor's body and personality. At that time there is an absence of personal persona and will, and that person is endowed with a supernatural presence and ability. Hurston touches one the role of the music and musicians, the praise services, order of worship and the Preacher. All of these are vital to penetrating and making contact with the spiritual realm.

Hurston felt that the Black preachers were the best poets and griots (or story tellers) of the culture. She thought they were masterful storytellers, highly intelligent, and they packaged their craft with such flair and drama, that the audience had no choice but to say "I BELIEVE'!

Hurston noted the importance and function of the oral tradition, which continues to inform the African-American cultural expression, it is highly used in secular and non-secular settings. The inflections and similes in Black speech are what she thought made Black language so rich. African Americans make speaking a sort of game, where fun and intrigue are some of the objectives in the language. It is also a powerful way to make points and transmit information. Language, for Black people, is a major psychological force for catharsis, healing and release. It provides a cleansing in such a way that nothing else can. Words are then tools of transformation and inspiration. Language is a way of reaching a psychological climax or peak that Black people have recognized and used for ages.

The spoken word for Hurston provides a conceptual analysis in addition to the artistic expression. She felt that "God" was too great an artist to leave the Black people out of the artistic picture. Hurston, as a matter of fact, she used the historical, sociological and psychological aspect of African American life as added fuel in her discussion of this artistry. This ultimate spiritual high is another aspect that Hurston found profoundly interesting and moving, and spoke volumes about Black Culture.

Zora Neale Hurston has certainly been vital in giving respect and voice to the beliefs, ideas, and expression of Black Culture. Her intent was to assist in helping Black people understand and be proud of their lively, joyous, and colorful culture. Additionally, her work helped to establish African American life and folklore as a legitimate body of knowledge, and placed in on the literary map for other ethnic groups to learn from and to enjoy.

"SHE LAID HANDS ON THEM AND THEY DID RECOVER"

3

HEALING

Note to reader: At the end of this chapter you will be asked to maintain a prayer journal.

African People have discovered and utilized a number of healing methods such as the use of herbs and other healing plants, spiritual readings, and other forms of spiritual healing namely, shouting, testifying, sitting through a "church service" are among the ways in which the different healing modalities have proven beneficial and effective for unnumbered and untold generations and centuries. Healing is about directing and redirecting energy throughout the physical, psychological and spiritual planes. Healing is about purifying and releasing negative and sometimes destructive elements that often keep us in turmoil. The ultimate goal of healing is to foster wholeness, with balance serving as the equilibrium that keeps and maintains the "whole person". The thing that is to be made clear is healing is based on faith and love. Therefore healing can be transforming.

Our bodies are energy systems of intelligence and vibrations. These cognitions and creative sources can be regulated, tapped into and directed. They are also accessible for healing; for healing is a response to this magnificent energy exchange. The question then becomes "What are the organizing principles for bringing healing into manifestation"? A principle is an overview of a plan or how something works.

Below are some of the principles by which spiritual healing can transpire:

Anchoring—Anchoring is making contact with infinite intelligence (God) the "Source", the "All." Ultimate reality is the unifying principle that guides all things. The anchoring process is connecting with this reality and remembering and believing we are a part of a spiritual universe, and have input into the creative and healing process.

Visualization—One must see through his or her mind's eye this power radiating through the entire being. It can be visualized as a powerful light, activity or movement, or an overwhelming excitement. For others it can be embraced as the "still voice" or the "witness."

Shifting—Shifting involves a change in consciousness where he or she identifies with the source, wholeness, power, strength, and is willing to take their rightful place in the spiritual universe of oneness, connectivity and divinity.

Acceptance-This is the stage where one receives his or her healing, by believing it is done, it is finished, and I am healed.

African-Americans have used a number of primary remedies and methods for healing. Among them is the power of prayer; the laying on of hands; rituals; and herbs as ways to maintain and regain health and strength. Let us look at the laying on of hands for example.

The Laying on of Hands

The Laying on of Hands is a healing methodology that is known and used in some Black religious circles. It can be viewed as an example or form of spiritual energy work, where energy is transferred from one person to another. In this type of healing, the healer covers the person seeking healing with his or her own healing or energy. In fact the healer heals him or herself and holds the "sick" person with his/her energy.

The laying on of hands is also a healing art discussed in The Bible and therefore also a Judeo-Christian tradition. However African-Americans tend to use this tradition coming from the Holy Scriptures over most of all other traditions connected to this heritage. As recorded in Matthew 8: 3 "And Jesus put forth his hand and touched him saying. I will; be thou clean. And immediately his leprosy was cleansed." In Pentecostal and "full gospel" (Fundamental Baptist, Church of God, Church of God in Christ, Spiritual Baptist and Independent Baptists) churches, African Americans use the power of the "Holy Ghost" as (an) 'agency' by which they heal. On the other hand, in some of these churches, the Minister places his or her hands on the heads and foreheads of members as a way of healing through prayer after a segue from the "heat" of his sermon into their mode and means of healing. Here as with the other means, energy is crystallized in the hand and the hands are then conductors and transmitters of this abundant energy/soul outlet. In another instance, the laying on of hands is usually accompanied by a prayer, followed by then hands laid on the forehead.

Under the Eastern Practice of India placing the hand or hands on or near the forehead is referred to as the "third eye." The third eye is one of the Seven Chakras or spiritual or energy centers within the body. Chakras are used in various traditions as points of healing within the body. Other cultures have different names for this methodology, such as "Touch Therapy" i.e. Reiche, Massage, Healing Hands, etc. In some societies such as India and Japan, the body may not be touched, to encourage healing; the hands are merely placed close to various parts of the body.

Another Chakra or point of contact for the laying on of hands is the "Heart Chakra." This is considered the seat of the emotions. Many healers believe that emotional pain and distress can make the body sick; therefore, this center is generally included in a healing session involving the laying on of hands. On some occasions, the healer will use "Olive Oil" on the sick person. This is a part of the anointing process discussed in The Bible and other holy books. "Thou anointed my Head with oil, my cup runneth over."(23rd Psalms) African Americans put these three concepts together in a healing session. Touch, Prayer and Anointing with Oil.

The Healer may speak in tongues during the healing session and the sick person may pass out or be "Slayed in the spirit," where they temporarily lose consciousness. Sometimes they may shake or become dizzy. In the Christian faith, the Healer, on occasion, may make a definitive statement such as, "Be healed in the name of Jesus!" The person, being healed, may sit or stand, or kneel during the healing or energy exchange. The sick person may be asked to lay his/her hand on the ailing part of the body or may be asked to say or repeat something.

According to Christian and Hebrew teachings, the laying on of hands is first activated by faith in God. (The Creator or God has a name, Yahweh, Jehovah, Oludamare, Allah, etc). "Without faith one can do nothing" and a belief in the Healers ability to be used as a channel for healing. This ability is called a "gift." It is considered one of many available to children of faith or the body of believers.

Others are the gift of teaching, prophecy, discernment, music, etc., just to name a few.

The healer generally begins his/her sessions with a prayer of purification, thanksgiving, or a prayer of solicitation and invocation, where the spirit is invited to assist in the healing process. Sometimes the person desiring healing is given a power object consisting of a piece of cloth that has been consecrated to wear for a certain period of time.

Touch therapy is now considered very therapeutic and useful in scientific and healing communities. The work in neonatal units in various hospitals throughout the United States is now embracing the use of touch, with premature babies, and is discovering that human touch is life enhancing. Some have even described touch as being a "Human Requirement" necessary to sustain life and vitality.

On some occasions the Healer will recommend additional remedies as well, such as a prescribed drink, of which water is the most common. The sick person may be asked to drink a number of glasses of water, or use garlic or the aloe plant to assist the healing and purification process.

As we recall the various healing arts, some African-Americans must first heal their own negative conditioning regarding this methodology and beliefs about these sciences. We must be sure to record and remember these healing cures or these cures or methods will be lost. Healing is about relocating oneself with the larger scope of the cosmos and remembering who we are. We are spiritual beings living a physical life. All cultures have powerful resources that if explored may be utilized for health and well being, for spirit is universal.

PRAYER

Prayer has the tremendous power to radiate energy in all directions. It sets in motion a series of events. It has been said that "you cannot think certain thoughts without evoking a certain response." Prayer, in African cosmology, combines the power of faith, thoughts, words, and, very often, music. All of these are cosmic magnetic sources that unite and assist in bringing forth the invisible into physical manifestation. We live in an ocean of vibrating and electrically charged energy forces. (Blaze & Blaze)

Prayer activates the miraculous in our lives. Traditional African thought embraces nature-based religious systems. African ancestors intuitively understood the interconnectivity that unites all things. They were keen observers of the weather, the sky, and natural forces. They recognized these energy forces in animals, people, and the spirit world. It would be very easy for these animistic people to believe the idea of transferring one energy source to another. For many Africans, life is a walking prayer. They hold the belief that sacredness can exist in many domains of existence.

"Where attention goes, energy flows." Prayer is crystallized, concentrated thought. It is one's divinely focused and directed will. Prayer is a methodology that channels the flow of energy in a specific direction. Prayer is an act of faith, submission and love. Prayer is probably the most powerful and oldest of all spiritual disciplines. It is also the most misunderstood. Prayer transcends religion and culture, space and time. It belongs to all people and is at the heart of all spiritual ideologies and theologies. It binds people together as they seek to make contact with that "super-conscious force field that many refer to as God."(Blaze & Blaze)

Every word, thought, desire, sentiment, intention contains a quantum force field we call energy; every thought we have goes somewhere. A thought is not a non-entity, it moves; it has life, consciousness and energy. We swim in a sea of energy like a fish swims in water. We do not and cannot exist without it. It is part of what and who we are. The more we understand this principle, the better prepared we are to embrace prayer and utilize its power in our daily lives.

  a. When we pray, we activate electrical and vibration force fields that encompasses and envelopes us. Prayer gives us access to infinite intelligence and strength. It is the "hook up" with divine mind. When we pray we ignite a series of events, and several laws and principles are activated on our behalf. (Blaze & Blaze)

b.   The law of receptivity-"Give and it shall be given unto you. The desire and the act of prayer provide a channel whereby we receive. Giving of ourselves in prayer activates the law of receptivity. This is closely related to the law of cause and effect. When we give up our egos, give of our time, energy, and attention, we give of ourselves.

c.   The law of desire—The law of desire propels and sets in place motivation. Motivation means to "move" to direct energy in a specific direction. Desire is that rush of power that intensifies and moves this energy. Energy cannot be stifled nor stagnated when fueled with desire.

d.   The Law of love—Love is a mighty power. Love is pure light. There is no force that can stand in the face of love, for love cannot be conquered. Love cannot be denied. Love purifies and cleans our intentions and as a result fortifies and propels us.

e.   The law of Expectation—"And you will have whatever you say." Your intentions shape and cut into form and affect your thoughts and desires. Intentionality activates faith, and faith speeds up the process by cementing your intentions.

EXERCISE 1
Please write your own prayers in the Prayer Journal for the next seven (7) days.

"DREAMS ARE VISIONS OF YOUR INTERNAL AND EXTERNAL
WORLDS"

4

DREAMS

Note to Reader:
At the end of this chapter you will be asked to do an exercise on dreaming.

African-Americans, along with many other cultures, are profoundly interested and intrigued by dreams, which are often viewed as messages from God. Especially provocative are those inescapable and compelling "big dreams." When The Bible said, "Your young men shall see visions, and your old men shall dream dreams," this gave the Black church full liberty to explore their dreams, though African people have done so since time immemorial. In African American history, dreaming is a part of what Black people do and believe in. Consider Harriet Tubman and her work with the Underground Railroad. (Van De Castle) She noted that she received her routes and plans in dreams. Additionally, it is no accident or surprise that Martin Luther King had a dream; this faculty is deeply implanted in our cosmology. "Holy Men and Women in Africa would dream of remedies for the sick and those in despair (Fontana)."

African-Americans are especially concerned with the sacred or revelation dreams. A deceased family member may come in a dream with a warning or a directive. Revelations are also presented in dreams by those who are living as well. African cosmology holds that dreams are from a profound metaphysical source. A belief in clairvoyants and seers is prevalent in the culture. African-Americans believe that dreams can show you your future and your sins. If your life is out of order, dreaming is a way to restore order and psychological and spiritual equilibrium. It is also believed that dreams can be used to reveal healing methods for the ill and the dispirited. African people are firm believers that dreams are channels whereby the spirits speak. Additionally, dreams provide access to important information, and they also can teach and inspire. For some people, time does not exist in the dream world. Future, present, and past are mixed in such a way that everything is just one big now.

Are dreams a source of deep hidden knowledge, liken unto a sort of sixth sense? Are they random meaningless data, composed of images, thoughts and insignificant garbage that one collects and later discards during the night? Do dreams have any relevance to real life? These are some of the many questions asked. But they are also pervasive, and tend to summarize how many, particularly in" Modern Cultures" view dreams and dreaming.

This work upholds the position that dreams can be a bridge to understanding one's life and affairs. Additionally, dreaming can be a powerful and accessible link to the unconscious level of mind or spiritual domains of existence. This type of linkage is only possible when one understands the principles and possibilities available to them. It is vital that this type of realization and clarity is made on an individual or personal realm first and foremost. This is possible through experimentation (trail and error), faith, remembering and the by the establishment of understanding your own dream language. It is important to be able to interpret and become bilingual and conversant with this method of communication. This language is "Soul" language and can only be understood if one is in tuned.

A survey of the literature suggest that dreams can and have been useful in a number of ways and serves the following purposes:

1. Dreams can bring messages from the spiritual domain of existence.

2. Dreams can provide knowledge of future events.

3. Dreams can signal a need for change or needed development.

4. Dreams provide access to creativity and potential.

5. Dreams can inspire and encourage.

6. Dreaming is a way to contact the intuitive level of mind.

7. Dreams can allow one to find meaning, purpose and mission in life.

8. Dreams can provide warnings.

9. Dreams can allow for healing and curative methods.

10. Dreaming can provide a window into divine mind and consciousness.

11. Dreams can lead one into psychological and spiritual integration.

12. Dreaming is a way to vent, release, and sublimate frustration, anger and aggression.

13. Dreams can direct, instruct and guide.

14. Dreams are a methods to contact others, and for others to contact you.

15. Dreaming can allow for adventures and fun.

Scientists are now telling us that up to one third of our lives can be revealed in our dreams. The key variables are :(1) How does one access the dream to explore this inward journey? (2) What is the formula for decoding the dream? (3) How does one understand the interlocking relationships of our waking and dreaming lives? (4) How does one log into and become sensitive to the "force field" that informs all material and non material essence. The answers to these questions can be explored in a number of ways. One is through a historical, psychological, and sociological study of various cultural views and experiences.

Dreams and dreaming is a topic that has interested some, fascinated others and provided sound guidance and information to many throughout the ages. World cultures have long understood the significance of sleep and dreams. The ancient Greeks and Egyptians erected temples and shrines dedicated to sleep and dreaming. They viewed these temples as healing centers and as a result their sick would sleep there, because it was believed so deeply that healing or a healing solution could be obtained through dreaming. Some would be guided by priests at these centers in prayers and various ritual procedures such as invocations, chants, various water healings and purification baths, herbal methods, and periods of fasting.

In India, it was felt that prophetic dreams came to those who had made significant advancement in their soul or spiritual development. The Chinese felt that something deeply mystical occurred during sleep and held a belief that the soul travels to other worlds and dimensions during sleep. Dreams are mentioned in the old and new testaments. According to Judeo-Christian beliefs this is a method of how God speaks to man. In the Buddhist tradition it is felt that dreams can show you your faults as well as your sins.

Native Americans gave us the concept of the "Big Dream" and were so invested in dreaming that they constructed "Dream Catchers" to hold and retain the dream. In the country side of Haiti, a topic of conversation is "What Did You Dream Last Night"?

Many events have been foretold in a dream. Take for example the sinking of the Titanic, the assassination of President Abraham Lincoln, the death of Tupac Shakur, Hannibal's epic journey. Countless other events were given in dreams prior to their occurrences.

The Natural and Social Sciences can be useful in understanding and appreciating dreams. Psychologically speaking, Sigmund Freud's Psychoanalytical theory is partially based on Dream Analysis. For Freud, dreams provide a storehouse of information as they deal with and reflect a person's psychological issues and history. Carl Jung thought that dreams were important as well and a methodological to tap into the "Collective Unconscious", that vast universal storehouse of knowledge. Nathanial Kleitman and Eugene Aserinsky felt that dreams were so important, that they started the first Dream Laboratories, so that dreams could be studied clinically and scientifically.

Most scientists believe that one dreams during the REM stage. (Rapid Eye Movement.) Most dream specialists believe that all mammals dream, and hold that for newborn babies' dreams are probably their first languages. Many who are around newborns having observed them smiling and demonstrating a variety of behaviors during the REM stage. Dreaming involves stillness and a certain level or relaxation. When the brain waves begin to drop to the alpha stage, one begins to benefit from the release of healing and reinvigorating hormones. During this stage scientists believe that one begins to shift in and out of consciousness. The next drop is into the Theta stage, and most experts believe that it is this stage that most people dream. The final stage is the Delta stage, which is even a deeper level of relaxation. During this stage it is believed that one does not dream but the body is so still and relaxed it allows itself to be repaired and regenerated. Relaxation tends to be a major ingredient in dreaming, then healing and intuition processes can provide access to this domain.

Another way to access the dream is purifying ones "Intentionality." Inherent in the intention, is faith. One's belief system tends to set the parameters for the experience. With this component intact one can began to program the subconscious mind to firstly remember the dream, and then begin to put this level of consciousness to work on your behalf by beginning to ask it questions and allow it to engage in problem solving. Knowing the right questions to ask becomes very important to obtaining the right answer. This implies that one must be somewhat self aware. Psychologists hold that prophetic dreamers tend to have a higher I.Q. This realm is not for amateurs but holds that one should bring something to the "dreaming table" for it to work for you.

As one becomes conversant with their dreams an ongoing dialogue can be established. This can be done through journaling, letter writing, or discussing your dream with a "Dreaming buddy" or support group. This developing and ongoing relationship with yourself can be one of the most rewarding relationships ever.

One way to become conversant with your dreams is to understand your patterns. It is imperative that you can retrace the dream, what was the emotion, sensation, imagery, parallel, and synchronicity? Can you pair the experience? Were there any relationships established? Did the dream become actualized or true on some level? These are some of the parameters to use in prophetic dreaming. The conscious and subconscious minds must meet. How many times have you been dreaming, and you get a message from the conscious mind that you need to go to the bathroom, or wake up for other reasons. You sent your subconscious mind back a message: "Not yet!" Or you speed up the dream, or put in on "pause". This relationship with both levels of mind is possible, and operational in many cases.

To make the best of your dreaming potential you may consider engaging in the following:

(1) Prepare yourself—by clearing and cleaning your mind, body and spirit. Facilitate your space by making it as comfortable and relaxing as possible. If there are any wrongs you have done or been done by others, forgive.

(2) Relax yourself, be still, be quite, still yourself to receive and hear from the deep communications of your soul.

(3) Utilize your spiritual attributes: Have Faith, be patient, love and honor your creator, yourself and others.

(4) Be grateful that this opportunity is available to you. Gratitude opens one up to receive more, and more and more, until your cup overflows with bounty.

(5) If you have a particular problem or question ask for the answer: "seek and you shall find. Knock and the door will be opened for you"

(6) Pay attention to your attention and to the clues or answers given in your dreams.

(7) Record your messages: This can be recording in print or you may use of any technology you find useful.

(8) Enjoy yourself: Dreaming is a privilege and a divine opportunity. Enjoy your journey and your life!

EXERCISE 2

*PLEASE RECORD YOUR DREAMS FOR THE NEXT SEVEN (7) DAYS IN THE INCLUDED DREAM JOURNAL FOUND AT THE END OF THE BOOK.

A NEW SYNTHESIS …

5

THE NEW THOUGHT MOVEMENT

There are a growing number of African Americans who are attracted to the Christian New Thought Movement. This chapter explores and summarizes some of its concepts and beliefs.

For each of the world's major religions, there is a corresponding mystical tradition. The New Thought Movement is the mystical arm of Christianity. According to Charles Fillmore, founder of the Unity School of Christianity, New Thought is "A mental system that holds man as being one with God (good) through the power of constructive thinking" (*The Revealing Word*, 140).

Always inspired by her messages, I conducted an interview with Dr. Mary Tumpkin, a leader in the Christian New Thought Movement and gained tremendous insights from her.

The New Thought Movement offers an alternative to fundamental Christianity. It is the reinterpretation of Christian concepts, themes, ideas, and scriptures from a historical, practical, and personal perspective. New Thought Christians, like all mystics, seek individual communion with God. The Bible is studied allegorically as the universal story of humankind. This is a liberating theology that strives to understand an ultimate reality (GOD) that is good, omniscient, omnipresent, and omnipotent. New Thought shuns religious dogma in favor of principles for empowered living.

The New Thought Movement follows the teachings of Jesus, who is recognized as a "Way Shower" or model rather than as the Savior of traditional Christianity. According to New Thought, Jesus' message was one of peace and love, and it promoted the development of a personal relationship with God. Jesus taught that people had the power to tap into God for themselves, and during his life he demonstrated how this could be done. The New Thought Movement teaches that God is neither a person, place nor thing, but invisible energy which permeates all that is. The best possible description of God for the New Thought Christian is the "Absolute." Possible alternative words for God are Divine Mind, Being, Creator, Source, and Spirit.

Although the New Thought Movement began less than one hundred years ago in the United States, its true origin dates as far back as the Mystery Schools of Ancient Egypt and Ancient Greece. In fact, it embraces much of the scholarship, philosophical thought, and foundational ideas of various Eastern religions. Some early New Thought pioneers include: Phineas Parkhurst Quimby, who is generally credited as the father of New Thought. Quimby was born in New Hampshire and is remembered for his work in mental healing and his technique of hypnotism; Mary Baker Eddy, the founder of Christian Science, was a noted writer, thinker, and healer; Emma Curtis Hopkins was another contributor, and she was the founder of the Christian Science Theological Seminary in 1887; Charles and Myrtle Fillmore were the founders of the Unity School Of Practical Christianity; Ernest Holmes and his brother Fenwick started the Metaphysical Institute in 1917, and in 1926 Ernest published the book *Science of Mind*; Dr. H. Emile Cady was one of the first prominent writers of the Unity Movement, and she wrote clear lessons of healing.

The New Thought Movement draws from many roots, including Gnosticism (Christian Mysticism). Gnosis means "knowledge," and the Gnostics believed they were the bearers of the secret teachings of Jesus. The Gnostic Gospels are gaining visibility in contemporary society, especially since the discovery of the Gospel of Thomas in a cave in Nag Hammadi, Egypt in 1945. Among the Gnostics, women were just as important as men, and many women were profound teachers, priests, and healers. Many of the leaders of the contemporary New Thought Movement are, in fact, women.

Ancient Judaism, the mother religion of Christianity, is another strong root of New Thought. Judaism allows for the allegorical interpretation of the scriptures. The Jewish Mystical Tradition is called "Kabala," which means "tradition." Its ultimate goals are to get closer and closer to the one great essence and to understand that duality of knower and known does not exist—there is no separation at all. Kabalists practice yoga, utilize methods of breathing and concentration, and repeat mantras as methods of reaching spiritual revelation

The Buddhist tradition has made its mark on New Thought as well: the New Thought Movement embodies the "Eight Fold Path" that comes out of the Four Noble Truths of Buddhism. Although Buddhism began in India, it is rare there today. It has since moved east to Japan, China, Tibet, and other places within and around the Asian Diaspora.

Perhaps the oldest, most far-reaching roots of New Thought Christianity can be traced to the ancient Mystery Schools or Spiritual Universities of Alexandria, Egypt and Greece. The Mystery Schools arose from ancient Shamanic practices and involved the study of rational philosophy, music, and art. They were also the birthplace of science and mathematics. Pythagoras, the Father of Mathematics, was initiated into and studied in the Mystery Schools for twenty years. The famous saying "Know Thyself" was inscribed over the portals of the temples.

The Mystery Schools taught that life is a process of awakening. Masters stressed the importance of finding one's higher nature and the underlying oneness with God. In laymen's terms, they were interested in the development of the whole person. These schools accepted a personal and spiritual understanding of life that promoted integration, self realization, and self-actualization. Initiations stressed focus, concentration, study, readiness skills, and mastery, which were believed to be the keys to spiritual power and mind control. The masters understood the danger of mixing higher knowledge with unready minds and consciousnesses. Many of the same concepts can be found in the New Thought Movement today.

According to the Reverend Dr. Mary A. Tumpkin, President of the Universal Foundation for Better Living (an international association of New Thought Christian churches and study groups founded by the Reverend Dr. Johnnie Coleman in 1974), and Senior Minister of the Universal Truth Center in Miami Gardens, Florida, one of the missions of the New Thought Movement is to bring the female back to the Christian dialogue. Says Tumpkin, "New Thought is feminism in action." Another of the Movement's missions is to offer "a counter discourse to mainstream Christianity and a larger look at the Christian religion, other world religions, and spirituality in general. It does so by drawing of a divergent set of ideas and theoretical perspectives." Tumpkin encourages individuals to find their own unique truths as they search out God's plan for their lives.

"Ultimately, the New Thought Movement must work to build and establish a community of faith that upholds spiritual unfoldment, personal growth, equality, scholarship, and goodness," she says.

Dr. Tumpkin sees the New Thought Church as a response to the victimized and suffering church. "It offers itself as new model: an empowerment center," she adds. "No one should be discounted based on race, ethnicity, gender, religion, age, or sexual orientation. The New Thought Christian is a metaphysician—an explorer of Self and a teacher and student of the laws of Spirit."

"CALL FORTH THE PROPHETS ..."

6

THE MYSTICAL EXPERIENCE OF PROPHECIES

A prophecy is knowledge of an event or occurrence prior to it happening. This occurrence is a universal phenomenon and happens in all cultures, in all religions, and in all societies. This is a profound mystical experience, which has been documented throughout the world and throughout the ages. Various theories have been given to try to explain how this amazing gift transpires. Some believe that they are scenes from the sixth sense. Some think that this is a faculty of our brain, and those with extraordinary I.Q.'s can access this ability. Others believe that these are conversations and visions from the spiritual realm, that individuals in tune with that realm can pick up this energy, vibration or knowing. Those who have this ability are called prophets or seers in some black church traditions. Those, who have this ability outside of the church, are known as clairvoyants, mystics or psychics. I would like to discuss two who have had a profound impact on me. My experiences and my associations with them have caused me to be a convinced believer.

Queen Esther Hopkins

Queen is an African American woman now in her 70s. I met Queen at a church I attended in the 1980's, and served as an apprentice under her. She has been an evangelist and church worker for many years. She has a depth of "spiritual knowledge, and is a woman of many "good" works. She has had an active prison ministry, serving delinquent teens and young adults. Queen, without fail, would gather the "faithful" once a month to provide these youth a worship service. Every Christmas she, along with her following, would give these young people a wonderful holiday fest of turkey, dressing, collard greens, macaroni and cheese, cakes, pies, and all of the trimmings. At the end of dinner and of course a religious service. Queen would make sure that all of the children had a gift. Sometimes on Saturdays, after our regular prayer meeting, she would go out into the streets of Miami, Florida and feed the homeless and those in needs.

On the first day of every month she would call a three day fast. During the fast periods she (we) would have daily devotional services in our individual homes and not eat for most or all of the day. Occasionally, Queen would call a shut in. During the shut ins we would move into the church for an overnight period or for several days. This is a time of worship and no distractions of everyday life.

Queen believes in a life of abstinence, meaning no drinking or smoking, no sex outside of marriage, no gambling, clubbing, or backstabbing. She lives a clean life that is set aside for God's use. Her practice is to attend church on Tuesdays, Fridays, and Sundays, in addition to the worship service she has at her own home on Saturdays.

Queen routinely shouts and dances in the spirit, along with speaking in tongues. These are practices known well in Black Pentecostal Churches. She is a prayer warrior and has the ability to heal and cast out evil spirits. She is a highly anointed minister, who is good with words and provides thought provoking and moving sermons. As I assess her methods, I could draw the following conclusions about Queen:

1. She has and maintains a constant connection with the Divine.

2. She is motivated by love for "God" and for others.

3. She has a deep and abiding faith in God that is unshakable and unmovable. (Having a serious illness over 20 years ago, but refused medical treatment for it)

4. Queen is "active" a doer/worker.

5. Music, singing and dancing help to activate her spirit.

6. She engages in spiritual disciplines of prayer, fasting, shut ins, consecration, (meditation) and she constantly reads the Bible.

"The Prophetic Gifts from Queen"

At one point in my life, Queen knew I was deeply troubled and concerned about not being able to conceive children. I was married and 28-years old. Over four years passed and no baby. Queen said that she saw me in a vision with two sons. She added that one son had on a coat just like his fathers. I held on to her "vision" and sure enough, I gave birth to son number one, and 18 months later I had son number two who looks very much like his father. This prophecy gave me so much hope, encouragement and comfort in my time of despair.

"Mattie Rolle"

Mattie is an African American woman in her 50s. I initially met Mattie while attending Florida Memorial College in Miami Florida. I rented a room from her one summer. During this time her psychic gift was not apparent, at least not to me. Time went by and we stayed in contact off and on over the years and reconnected about five years ago and have stayed close friends.

I do not believe Mattie's gifts are totally church related even though she attends church from time to time. Mattie does have some spiritual disciplines however. She will fast, pray, and eat a light diet. She uses focus, concentration, and her hearing abilities to interact with the spirit world. Mattie told me that the spirits have personalities; some are very funny. Some of the spirits that surround Mattie enjoy listening to James Brown and request she plays his music in her car. Some of the spirits are children, and they love to go with Mattie when she is visiting a home where other children live.

Mattie indicated that her gift was triggered by a number of events e.g., her father's death, the handwriting of others, from which she had "knowledge about them." and she had premonitions of airplane crashes prior to them going down. She has the ability to look through another person's eye and tell them what they are looking at. For example, she told me early in our reconnection period that I had black sheets on my bed. On another occasion, while talking on the phone, she told me that I had a gold shoe that was out of alignment in my closet. Wow, from that point on I became a believer, but this was only the beginning.

She informed me one day while in conversation at my house that she saw me with a vacation home, in New England, and not to worry about the money it would come to me. Sure enough I found a vacation home in Massachusetts, and a family member (whom I quickly repaid) loaned me $20,000 for its purchase.

She also told me I would get a car to keep in the area where I have my house. I received a very good deal on a Volvo from a preacher in upstate New York. Additionally, I received some free furnishing and dishes, just like Mattie predicted.

Mattie told me on another occasion that one of my sons was interested in getting "Gold Teeth." I approached both sons about it; they denied their interest, but later I found the imprints for the gold teeth in the glove compartment of my car, where he forgot to remove it.

On another occasion, Mattie told me to go to the doctor because I had an infection. Little did I know I had an infection, my doctor gave me a prescription to clear it up immediately with some antibiotics.

Mattie informed me on another occasion that "You will be working with top students." Shortly after that prediction, I was asked to be a founding faculty member for the Honors College at Miami Dade College. She also said that I would travel across a great body of water. Soon after that I was given the honor to travel to Germany and Austria for a Conference on Global Citizenship.

One night, over the telephone, Mattie told me to check my tires. When I did one of my tires was almost flat. I was barely able to make it to the service station. She told me on another day to check my wallet and keep my papers secure. Soon after her warning, I discovered that someone was using two of my credit cards.

Mattie told me one day, "The Spirits told me to tell you to drop" and she asked me "What does drop mean to you." Through my employment, there is a program called Deferred Retirement Option Program (DROP) that I was eligible to join. Since signing up, I have made a good bit of money. (Smile)

On a sad note, one day Mattie said to me, "I see death in her family." She was speaking to me about a friend in New York. A few weeks later, a close family member of hers died. And on a much lighter note, Mattie advised me that some of my students were passing notes around; these notes were on my upcoming midterm exam. I was able to change the test to maintain the integrity of the grading process.

These experiences along with others have given me a deep respect for the "Spirit World" and "True Seers". These gifts can prepare us for up coming events, help us to discover our potential, help minimize problems, and provide comfort in times of need.

"A DIFFERENT FRAMEWORK!"

7

EXPLORATION OF THE AFRICAN WORLD & AFRICAN AMERICAN THOUGHT

African American thought and African American spirituality are based on a variety of beliefs and approaches to life and anchored in a profoundly spiritual realm of existence. Many of these convictions or acceptances of truth have their origin in African Thought and African spirituality. According to Neimark in his work "The Way of the Orisa" African thought embraces a concept of oneness and integration. It does not separate logic and intuition, linear and non linear, theory and practice, spiritual and physical, body and soul (Neimark 5).

It embraces a philosophical view of extreme flexibility, improvisation, and spontaneity, which is consistent with an enriched spiritual life and belief (faith) that the Creator is in control and all is right and good. Because many of these barriers, labels, distinctions, and paradigms do not exist in African thought, African ways may be considered irrational, native, and primitive. In fact, this is how they are described by many in the literature. This is because it is hard to describe what you don't know. It is a different way of knowing and being that may be antithetical to others.

European thought and African thought have divergent streams of consciousness or points of divide that distinguish them. These points of departure allow for a whole range of expressions and manifestations in the African/African American Spiritual Experience. African thought allows for cultural and religious ways of engagement that are highly expressible and interactive i.e., spiritual possessions, dancing in the spirit, prophetic dreams, spiritual healings, and deep and profound revelations that some would consider highly unnatural or very strange.

One way to describe this structure of belief is that Black people tend to be very comfortable using both hemispheres of the brain—one part that embraces logic, order, structure, facts, and numbers, and the other part that draws on intuition, inspiration, feelings, emotions, faith, and creativity. As a result, African people tend to have an eclectic approach to life, blending and mixing what is viewed as contradictory elements together. In African thought, this type of synergy is holistic and natural. This fusion of attributes has provided for a spiritual and natural cosmology that allows Black people the mental freedom to persevere, to dance, sing, and be happy in the midst of seeming chaos. There is an old African American saying that expresses this view: "Everything is everything." This quote speaks volumes as it relates to the acceptance of the divine and natural order of things. It is an affirmation that, in a spiritual sense, all is well.

In African thought for example, one does not move to the spirit world upon death. African people believe that this is a spiritual world and that after people make their transitions they simply experience a different and deeper domain of that spiritual existence. A neighbor from Jamaica recounted her life in the country side of Jamaica where close relatives are buried in the front yard and her grandmother would have conversations with the ancestors several times a day. Africans believe that the soul never dies and the ancestors are still part of the family that one can consult for advice and help on the earthly plane. As a result of this view, African people live in the spirit, are receptors of information and divine revelations, and are beneficiaries of their spiritual existence.

African thought is *present* oriented, not *future* oriented. This view is based on experiencing the here and now—not someday. This might explain the concept of "colored people's time" (CPT); they operate on a totally different rhythm and view of time. What is important to many African people is what they are doing now, whether they are enjoying it, and whether it is necessary. This determines largely whether the activity will continue or be suspended. This aspect of African life is very much misunderstood. At times this is problematic when Africans come in to contact with present oriented cultures. This view of time orientation is also related to the notion of African people resisting the idea of saving for a rainy day or making funeral plans in advance.

African People are communal, not individualistic. This is made evident by many of the activities that Black people engage in such as partying and clubbing, and the fact that church membership and attendance is high in the African American communities. These services are highly active and participatory as opposed to distant and passive. Black people tend to be highly collaborative, consulting with family or friends before any major decisions are made. The fact that they are seekers of advice and opinions speaks to the participatory nature of this people and the levels of support and mutual aid upon which they have to draw. For many, this allows for a deep level of emotional security. Relationships are highly valued, and Black people often address their peers as brothers and sisters and use special titles for sacred relationships, e.g., "my homeboy." This mind set and communal engagement has set the stage for a religious cosmology that is integrated, communal, participatory, and highly flexible. Additionally, this view has allowed for a deeply esoteric and penetrating religious expression that is built upon relationships on all levels of existence, both natural and supernatural.

The kinship ties are very close in Africa. For example, in the Yoruba communities in Africa, your cousins are considered your brothers and sisters. They also believe that you have more than one father. For example, your uncle (mother's brother) is also considered your father. This extended care and multi-leveled relationship is believed to be very psychologically healthy. Mutual aid and mutual support has been a very valuable asset and has provided for individual and cultural continuity. (Bass)

African people see life as a continuum, and in many parts of the Diaspora, ancestor reverence has provided for this view. Life is cyclical, and everything is connected. This practice is a way to hold the community together and to link the living with the ancestors. There is also a belief in the Yoruba Tradition that the Orisas (Spirits) live within us. It is also held that we should make the spirit as happy or as comfortable as possible. Music and drumming are some ways in which this is done. The Yoruba tradition also teaches that humans are not born of sin or of guilt. It is non-judgmental and holds that the ultimate goal of life is to learn transcendence. (Mark)

It is also noted that in Nigeria mental illness is dealt with in a whole different way. The mentally ill are integrated into the community and treated as normal. This high level of tolerance and flexibility has provided for stability and for the general well being of all. The missionaries also made the mistake of thinking that the African healers were witch doctors. Now many in the psychological field are using Freudian approaches such as "talk cures," free association, and, additionally, behavior modification methods that were once thought of as illogical in earlier times. It was also noted that as modernization increased in Africa, so did depression, anxiety, and general unhappiness. (Bass)

African science and African spirituality can be judged on these bases: "Does it work?" and "How does it work?" This "test of the hypothesis" is the true test of scientific method. If it does not work, the process starts over again, until the hypothesis is tested and proven. For people of African descent, they are well satisfied with the outcome of their methodologies and practices. As a result, their practices and beliefs are institutionalized and maintained.

African thought and spirituality hold a very high regard for the supernatural and nature. Africans believe that one can be cured by leaves, and that ones dreams can be analyzed by looking into fire, and that by invoking the spirit of trees, animals and people, lives can be transformed. (Bass)

African-Americans have adopted and modified an Africanized form of meditation. This practice is called "chillin'." This is a time of disengagement and relaxation, where work, toil, and worry are suspended. During the chillin' period, one may just lie in bed, or sit at home, in the yard, or with a close friend and do nothing. This form of non-doing is used in many cultures as a method of letting go and release. Additionally, this relaxation technique allows for:

a.   rest

b.   restoration of psychological equilibrium

c.   harmony

d.   mood adjustment or readjustment

e.   lowered blood pressure

f.   slowed heart rate

g.   creativity

h.   overall sense of well-being

The practice of chillin' is imperative for connecting Black people to their higher selves. This quiet time allows for improved health and wholeness. Medical research has provided some astounding data as it relates to quiet time. This is when one shuts down for 15-20 minutes, and the brain waves shift to the alpha state. When this shift occurs, the brain triggers the release of endorphins. This chemical, also called the "happy hormone," helps us fight infections, calms us down, and gives us a sense of tranquility. Silence has long been considered a methodology for spiritual well being. Others cultures call it "going into the silence" or meditation. Spiritually, the following benefits can be derived from chillin':

a.   increased receptivity to a divine message

b.   clearer sense of purpose

c.   enhanced power and strength

d.   greater centering effect in the midst of difficulty

e.   increased capacity to love

From a spiritual point of view, this form of meditation allows for the embrace and alignment of the spiritual presence. In a quiet state, one learns how to wait, exercise patience, and embrace the rhyme of life and the sequencing of events. Chillin' can provide a solid place to return for grounding and re-evaluation. It is here one can regain faith, perspective, and energy.

Ultimately, chillin' is about letting go. It is about waiting and resting. This renewal process helps to minimize the wear and tear on the body, mind, and spirit. It regenerates the soul. Solitude prepares us for work, and work prepares us for solitude. It helps you to understand when it is necessary to speak and when it is necessary for silence. Balance is key in these areas.

Stress is mental and physical strain. It comes about when one is overwhelmed by the feeling of having to cope with more than one can comfortably handle. It is believed that up to 98% of our diseases may be stress related. Stress threatens the stability of relationships, the health of the body, and the peace of the soul.

Chillin' allows us to go back to the source in which we can experience the primal forces that govern and regulate all things that encompass space, time, and existence. This methodology helps us to know ourselves within a larger context, as part of an infinite chain of existence. We have a vital and significant role to play on this magnificent stage of life, and we must allow ourselves the time to "Be still and know that I am God."

Again, African people are spiritual people, whether in a church, school, or nightclub. Wherever they are, a spiritual essence (God-force) can be felt and manifested. It is incumbent upon the Black church and other social intuitions to tell the truth and allow for a reunion with the cultural self. Africanisms are clearly exhibited and demonstrated in the shouting, spirit possessions, music, dance, spiritual drama, and rhythmic catharsis found in the Black church, as well as the power that accompanies these expressions. The African American church can be a wonderful source for understanding this spiritual legacy and the customs, habits and styles of Africa. It has been hundreds of years since African ancestors first came to this country, yet many still have the impulse to shout and to rejoice. (Asante)

In the process of coming home and coming to terms with African spiritual history, one can minimize double consciousness, neurosis, and cultural schizophrenia. There are living institutions within the community, i.e., the family, the church, and the school. If these institutions will accept the responsibility and rise to the occasion, they can assist their members with restoration to cultural and spiritual health, healing, and wholeness. The restoration of cultural truth will allow for greater access to the spiritual power that has made for a strong, powerful, and transcendent people.

AFRICAN AMERICAN THOUGHT: THE ISSUE OF "DISSING"

You have probably heard the expressions, "Don't mess with a Black man (or woman)," or "Don't touch that," or "Don't go there." These expressions are very instructive and are important aspects of African American life as it relates to the Sacred Codes of Conduct. African-Americans have drawn invisible lines in the sand. These marks of distinction and demarcation are known and understood in the culture as "the untouchables." They are behaviors that you just don't do or engage in, because these things can cause great offense. Sometimes these offenses or violations can cause permanent harm or damage. These major transgressions for many may be considered unforgivable. As a result, one may be "read" or told off, banished physically or emotionally (told, "You have to go,") or offered as a human sacrifice to the "gods."

Some of the most pronounced violations are as follows, and are referred to in this piece as the "African American Five Commandments":

1. Thou shall not dis(respect) one's family.

2. Thou shall not dis(respect) one's friends.

3. Thou shall not dis(respect) one's honor.

4. Thou shall not dis(respect) one's confidence.

5. Thou shall not dis(respect) one's money.

"Dissing" or disrespecting is a sin in the African American School of Thought. This behavior must be understood and regarded in everyday interaction, if things are going to "go right." Things "going right" in the culture largely depends on keeping the Five Commandments in everyday life.

The first commandment is *Thou shall not dis one's family*. Sayings such as, "Don't talk about my mama" (and this can apply to other family members as well), speak to the respect and honor given the black mother and family. Black people make this a point and a priority in their daily lives. There is a special bond that exists within the Black family. The family has been the buffer against a very harsh and hard world. The Black family has provided shelter from the storms of life, and security (both emotional and financial). As a result, one's family is off limits against anything that would be considered harmful or negative. The violation of family is cause for a great retribution.

The second commandment is *Thou shall not dis one's friends*. A friend in Black life is an extended family member—the family that people choose for themselves. In the Black community, one's friend is usually embraced by one's family. It is common knowledge that your friend is your family's friend. So by taking on a good friend, you automatically inherit a whole family. It is understood that a friend can eat at the table, go in the refrigerator (sacred ground), and be counted on to provide help in the time of need.

The third commandment is *Thou shall not dis one's honor*. That means not to "bad mouth," "show out," or make someone look bad in the eyes of others. African Americans are very communal and social and operate within a network of family, friends, and associates. To disrespect someone within their community by breaking them down publicly is considered a horrible offense, and it will not be taken lightly. Shaming and dehumanizing behavior is off limits. (There was enough of that during slavery and segregation.) African Americans hate to be embarrassed or brought down in front of others. "Make me look good" is a mantra that is secretly (or not so secretly) repeated in the African American community.

The fourth commandment is *Thou shall not dis one's confidence*. Translation: Don't tell my secrets. This commandment has to do with the trust factor. Trust is a very important aspect in the Black community. "I got your back" is an expression that is known in the African American community and implies a great deal of trust.

The fifth commandment is *Thou shall not dis one's money*. African Americans believe that they work hard for their money. It is true that many Blacks earn or receive less than the Anglos do for the same work, and they also face discrimination in hiring practices. African Americans provided free labor for so many years in this country that now being able to earn money demonstrates human and social justice. Money to African Americans is very important subject and symbolizes a great struggle and a much needed means to an end. African Americans will loan you money if you are a close friend or relative but will be quick to tell you, "Don't play with my money." How you handle a Black person's money will determine whether you get any more.

These sacred commandments should be honored and remembered. Failure to do so will meet with great repercussions. Black people are deeply emotional, highly verbal, and, as quiet as it is kept, very sensitive. To understand Black people and to maintain good relationships, one should take great care in honoring and obeying the Five Commandments.

"BLACK MUSIC CALLS FORTH YOUR "PARTICIPATION"

8

AFRICAN AMERICAN MUSIC & AFRICAN AMERICAN MOVEMENT

Please note at the end of the book you will be asked to keep a music log.

Music, like religion, is the African American dynamite. (Power source). Music gives the Black soul life and vitality. The richness of this music has worldwide notoriety and has given the world fascinating music, including Jazz which has been proclaimed by Congress as a National Treasure. What has made African American music so rich and so special? Why are the producers of this music so talented and profound? What does this music do for, or how does it impact its listeners? These are some of the questions that will be addressed in this section.

Generally speaking, to African people, music is a vital expression of life itself. Black music is alive, highly creative, and intensely emotionally charged. This music is sung and played from the soul; hence, the notion of "Soul Music," which has its origin, and speaks to this very point.

African music is a form of freedom and release. It allows one to be unbound and free in their emotions and feelings. Emotions such as joy, sorrow, pain, love, hope, and anger are expressed without boundaries or restrictions. It is raw, uncut, unedited, real, and an outflow of the depths of human feelings. This music tells the truth, and causes introspection; it is therapy—it heals you where you hurt. This music has a way a penetrating the inner most core of a person, thereby leaving the feeling of being transformed and transfixed.

The essence for African American life is found and embodied in its music and religion. These two aspects of Black culture, intersect, blend, and complete each other to such an extent that, at times, it is difficult to separate the two.

Black music serves individual as well as group functions. It is highly interactive and participatory in nature, and causes people to be bonded emotionally together in a profound and meaningful way. The music has been essential in maintaining group cohesiveness and group continuity (Kinney).

Music making and performing is a multi-dimensional process. It includes body movements, facial expressions, involves style and dress, is emotionally potent, and declares an internal presence that is inescapable. All of this combines with the music and serves to communicate with its audience and give an overall appeal (Kinney).

The unique sounds created by the Black performer demonstrate a large repertoire of musical interpretation. Black audiences demand much from their musicians in terms of musical aesthetics. A high level of mastery is required and expected. This is a "giving" from the very depths of one's being. It is an authenticity and a genuineness that cannot be faked or manufactured, or copied; it comes from the spiritual realm of one's existence. Spirit cannot be quantified or measured, it must be experienced.

African Americans interpret, develop and react to music out of a frame of reference that is largely African. As a result, Black music throughout the Diaspora is unified and further expresses the African continuity. Music remains at the core of daily life.

During slavery, missionaries had disdain for secular music calling it "Devil's Music." For a while these musical abilities were outwardly geared toward sacred music. "The Slave Spirituals were so powerful; one became overwhelmed by their intensity. Also included in the music were secret meanings encoded for meetings and escapes planned. It is believed that the power of the music allowed for a large degree of psychological and spiritual comfort during very dark and difficult days.

Black Music has its own dynamic which include metaphor, instruction, resistance, pedagogy, codes of expression and generally include an open ended dialogue. The singer may shout, whistle, yell, or groan, and may present a full range of sounds and behaviors (Hunter) Black Music is "So Funky" it makes you want to move your body. It appears in many cases that the musician understands how to interact, communicate and respond to the spirit and human world.

African Americans music is intense; the musician tends to come from very profound places emotionally and mentally. The music may grow out of great joy, pain, or a need to express and to create. It is an outgrowth of the African and American-American psychic that has a special and heightens sensibility and experience:

The musician is a talented, cultural worker and translator of spirit and envelops a number of qualities and attributes:

-High levels of creativity
-Strong sense of rhythm, timing, and balance
-Discipline
-Dedication to their craft
-Serious in their desire to pursue their endeavor
-Open to be a receptor of creative inspiration

Musicologists tell us that music in general can have positive effects on the psychological, physical, and cognitive functioning. Music has amazing effects on the behavior of children, the elderly and those with a variety of mental health needs and those in pain.

It appears that music for the most part is a human need and human requirement. It is a universal phenomena that transcend culture and condition that has proven useful in most if not all parts of the world.

Music serves the following purposes and provides the following benefits:

-It aids in stress reduction
-It improves communication skills
-It enhances motor skill
-Improves memory and concentration skills
-Elevates self understanding and self growth
-Allows for unspoken emotions
-Expresses feelings

-Allows for sublimation or channeling of emotions

Music Therapy

Trial and error and experience is the best way to know how music affects you. One approach to implementing your own personal music therapy is by maintaining a music log or journal and keeps a list and record that include but not limited to the following:

a.   Music that give me a lift.

b.   Music that helps me when I am physically ill.

c.   Music that minimizes my stress.

d.   Music that provides encouragement.

e.   Music that helps me releases my pent-up emotions.

f.   Music that helps me to relax.

g.   Music that makes me want to move.

h.   Music that makes me feel joyous.

i.   Music that connects me to the divine source.

j.   Music that facilitate meditation.

k.   Music that improves concentration.

l.   Music that heighten romantic emotions.

m.   Music that minimizes romantic emotions.

n.   Music that motivates me.

o.   Music that calms me down.

p.   Music that aids in pain reduction.

q.   Music that minimizes depression.

r.   Music that opens me up emotionally.

s.   Music that closes me down emotionally.

By maintaining a music log, the music that suits your individual needs will be readily available to you whereby can be utilized in time of need. Additionally, it will assist in minimizing your discomfort and provide the remedy necessary.

Music is a universal gift and privilege, don't neglect the opportunity to heal yourself and make yourself feel better. Music is a proven cure, so let the music play on!

EXERCISE 3

- RECORD THE MUSIC YOUR LISTEN TO FOR THE NEXT SEVEN (7) DAYS. REFLECT ON YOUR MOOD AND HOW THE MUSIC AFFECT YOUR MOODS AND EMOTIONS.

African Americans & Movement

For African people, movement tends to be highly essential: It is almost as if African People have to move. Parents, teachers, and others who are in constant contact with African American youth, and African people in general, would be able to understand them better, and the quality of their interactions and relationships would be strengthened if they could put this phenomena within a workable and useful framework.

Movement for Africans and people of the African Diaspora appear to be generated by a deep mental and physical strength and energy source that is difficult to quantify, but the manifestations are apparent. I say mental strength because the mind tells the body what to do. Black people move when they talk, eat, think, and are emotional. This is a major way in which they express themselves. Movement is clearly, a language for people of African descent. Many people within the culture have the ability to read this unspoken language. The "cool walk" or 'pimping' is an example. The Black woman with her hand on her hip when she wants to make a point is another example of this cultural body language. When African Americans are upset one can tell if one "rises up." During the 'raising period' the stance and body movements actually rises up a level or two, and someone reading this behavior knows that someone has just crossed the line of what is considered acceptable behavior. There is also certain sensuality that accomplices African American Movement; it is highly seductive, and it is movement that speaks without speaking. From these movement patterns, one may gain information and input about a person and their feelings and intentions. One is encouraged to use additional methods, such as verbal and auditory skills for verification of those feelings and intentions however.

Africa has been long recognized for dance and its dancers. Dancing seems to make Black People happy, as expressed in R. Kelly's musical selection "Happy People." There have been accounts of Africans having danced so long and so intensely that they pass out. African people dance in all parts of the world—whether in Africa, the United States, Trinidad, Jamaica, Haiti, Cuba, Toronto Canada, the Virgin Islands, London England, Brazil, you will find some of the most prolific dancers in the world. This rhythmic heritage tends to be passed on to the future generations. It is not uncommon to see babies, even before they can walk in their parent's arms dancing. Older children are often observed learning the most popular dance form. So many of them are "born dancers." Many African Americans live for the weekends because "that's when they party down." Older people dance, or "Get their groove on." Religious people dance, they call it the "holy dance," but dance, never the less. It is as if they are able to go into a special "Zone" as they move.

Spirit Possessions or (Trance) is closely related to movement; it is in many cases, a primary method for entering a spiritual or mystical realm. Generally, the spiritual leader will request some type of movement before this spiritual peak can be obtained. It may be to stand and clap your hands as an opener. The hands are one's personal drums, where rhythm and movement can be united. From this movement comes 'the shout' and 'holy dance,' finally the spiritual trance. Movement again, acts as a trigger for this powerful manifestation, which is known largely throughout the African world.

This movement has served Africans well and exemplified by them being the number one runners throughout the world in long distance marathons. Their stamina and endurance is mind boggling. The fact that African Americans, while only about 12% of the United States Population, tend to dominate major sports. Sports such as basketball, boxing, football, baseball, now tennis and golf have been touched and greatly impacted by the "Black Athlete. How can these phenomena be explained? What parallels, models or inferences can be drawn? Suffice it to say in this piece that there are some special attitudes, attributes, skills and tendencies that live within the African Soul.

Movement is actually very healthy, and many benefits can be derived from movement and exercise:

    a.   It improves coordination

b. It strengthens the mind and body

c. Delays the aging process

d. Allows for more energy and stamina

e. Provides more pleasure in life

f. Helps to maintain weigh control

g. Tones the muscles

h. Burns calories

i. Improves self confidence

j. Vitalizes the system

k. Improves cholesterol level

l. Lowers blood pressure

m. Improves the appearance

While movement is important to many people, it is interesting and insightful how various African groups and cultures have expanded and amplified it into a beautiful skill and art form. A study or review of African American Movement can foster a greater awareness and understanding of African American culture and its African retentions.

SISTER GIRL!

9

THE AFRICAN AMERICAN FEMALE: A PSYCHO/ SPIRITUAL PERSPECTIVE

An exploration of the psychological makeup of the African American female is a topic that has received far too little attention in the literature. This type of analysis and discussion would add so much to a better understanding of the issues and methods of constructing and interacting with the African-American Female's "Emotional Self." One may be able to draw from this construct and use it as a source of empowerment that can be tapped into and used as a mechanism of transformation. Certainly the Black female and her experience is a testimony of power and inspiration that can be truly beneficial to the human experience. It is no doubt that she is strong and powerful. However, in the process of "making things happen," conquering worlds, and mastering universes, many times the black woman neglects herself.

The purpose of this analysis is to explore the historical evolution, coping strategies, psychological strengths, psychological challenges and potential methodologies for health and enrichment. Before exploring any topic of the psychology of the African American woman, there must first be a realization that she is a highly complex, diverse and multi faceted human being who is coming from divergent places regionally, emotionally, financially, and experientially. There are some common threads and perspectives that bind black women. There are issues that have grown out of common experiences that inform black women's behavior that is worthy of common reflection and hopefully, can be addressed positively as they move into the future.

As we examine the Black female experience, one must be cognizant of finding linkages and connections between theoretical paradigms to conceptualize a psychological strategy that would aid in an understanding of self. The ancients have long admonished us to do so from the famous affirmation: "Know Thyself." After that examination has occurred, it is then our responsibility to make the necessary adjustments. Thus it will allow for the restoration or formulation of psychological equilibrium, health and harmony to life.

Historical Evolution

When examining some of the historical tenets that have influenced the Psychological Development of Black Women a few themes come to mind:

a. Objectification

b. Subjectification

c. Segregation

d. Integration

Let us begin with the theme of objectification as it bears imprint on the psyche of the Black Woman. Objectification is one of the major historical struggles for the African American Woman and African Americans in general. Being objectified by the plantation owners (and society in general), employers, their men and sometimes even their children. "Mom, what are we going eat"?" I need this." "I want that." "Part the Red Sea for Me." While for the most part, they absolutely, adore, and value their children, men, and friends, but to be viewed as a 'Black Female VERSION of Santa Claus, is both taxing and insulting.

In the church setting, women pray more, attend church more, and give more than men. For the most part however, churches and religious institutions are headed by men. Sometimes it must feel that "Women gave their lives for the church." For this reason a reexamination of all our institutions is necessary in order to address the objectification of women.

Karl Marx in his critique of social arrangements and social structures reminds us of the question: "Who benefits from this arrangement?" after this question is honestly answered, one can take it from there. The larger question is who is in control here? It is a woman's right not to be disrespected, disregarded, and objectified. An Affirmation is needed at this time: "My body, my time, my labor, my sexuality, my mind and my essence belong to me. (and the Creator)
'NO MORE SLAVE MASTERS PLEASE'

The Black Female has experienced subjectification as well, which views women has a sort of label or topic, with no validity, feelings, or essence, "The Woman," "Mama" "My Girl", "That B" This approach to dealing with or addressing African American Women is dehumanizing and robs her of her true worth.

Women are thus objectified by (some) Black Men. Popular culture and media reveal numerous examples. Take this phrase from a former popular song "Shake your as_ shake it fast." These serve as mirrors to what is happening in society, and give us a glimpse into our relationship patterns as it relates to being viewed as objects by Black Men.

The period of Segregation said to African Americans you are not good as others (Whites) and sent a deep and painful message into the psyche of Black Folks. The Black Female being a double "minority" has had to endure a whole range of issues and psychological adjusting to maintain any sense of dignity, worth, and self respect. Many of the stressors, problems in relationships, and imbalances have grown out of a very demeaning and hurtful past, which will continue to plague her unless these issues are both understood and resolved.

In the early days of Integration, there was a continuous sense of not being wanted. Being perceived as a problem, an imposition, a burden, and down right hated, this could not have done much to boost the African Americans sense of self. Many had to dig deep into their resolve to cope with and overcome the nasty looks and comments, along with the humiliation and the disrespect presented to them. Some residual affects of all of this is still present today in various aspects of society. When considering all of this, one must honestly say, that Black People are not only strong but truly miracles.

Coping Strategies and Mechanisms

The Black Woman draws on a number of strategies and mechanisms to give her a sense of psychological well being. God, Jesus, Allah, Odumare, and all of our religious institutions, for ages have served as our strength and refuge. Black women find their way to church on Sunday or Saturday to turn their problems over to Jesus to work them out for us. For too long, psychological treatment was not available to Black People, when this option was available, Black people in general tended not to trust the psychological profession. Black people tend to go to God for help.

Other sources of Psychological help for the Black Female are the extended family: Mothers, Sister/Friends, who have served as a sense of comfort and aid in difficult times. Many of these women are truly brilliant in terms of their natural ability to counsel, make you laugh, console, and even take you out at the right moment.

Unfortunately, many Black Women engage in unhealthy defense mechanisms. A defense mechanism is a weapon used by the ego, to serve as protection from self created anxiety. The mechanism repression: The blocking of painful experiences and thoughts from consciousness. This mechanism serves to block out painful episodes and unpleasant feelings during slavery and the post slavery experiences. Some things were just too hard to bear. As a result Black People drew on this mechanism to help get through each day. The continuous use of it however, does not allow for resolution, and remains and later becomes pain and neurosis. Another defense mechanism used by the Black Female is the defense mechanism termed Denial. Many Black Women deny their pain, problems with our men, our children, and our health. Again, when issues remain unaddressed, they revisit us later. Black women also engage in rationalizing, or intellectualizing, where they begin to explain away certain behaviors. Coming largely from an oral tradition, this is easy to do. Black people tend to talk a lot, as they try to make sense of their world and experiences.

On a positive note, Black Women use the mechanism Sublimation. Sublimation is channeling primal impulses into positive, constructive efforts. A Black Woman can "make a way out of no way;" Turn lemons into lemonade. Some hold that the Black Women has the "Superwoman Complex." Sometimes however she should cross that "S" off her chest and just chill.

Personality Types

1. THE SUPER-HERO-This woman can jump tall buildings with a single bounce. She is all things to all people. She buys the bacon and cooks the bacon. The Super-hero is a very high achiever; she is in fact an over-achiever. She goes non-stop all day long. She is called on by her boss, family and friends, people she knows and people she does not know. Her phone mail, email, and appointment book is constantly filled. Her life is scheduled out. She has to almost make an appointment with herself just to get some sleep.

2. THE SAVIOR-The Savior is somewhat like the Super-hero, the difference between the two is that the Superhero is all things to all people and the Savior is all things to people in her inner circle. She should have been nailed to the cross, in that she is willing to give here life for others. She is a true martyr. She runs all around town doing errands and projects for others. She loans out money to family and friends in need. She cooks meals for holidays and other events. She should have been named "call on me". This woman is a sacrificer of the highest order. When ever there is an unmet need, or a problem to be solved, you can call on the Savior.

3. The Spiritual Guru—This woman has generally been raised in the church, temple, or mosque. She has studied the scriptures, has fasted and prayed, and dedicated a large portion of her life to God. She practices the spiritual disciplines of her faith and provides hope, advice and deliverance to others. This woman has been highly influenced by her culture and religion is and has been a large part of who she is.

4. The Scholar-This woman gets great joy from retiring quietly with a good book. She loves to read, study, and explore new ideas. She gets great personal satisfaction in knowing what is going on. She is deeply interested in those aspects of life that can transform her life. She makes her intellectual life bright and stimulating.

5. The Saturday Night Girl—She loves to party. This woman can be counted on to help lift your mood and change your perspective by a night on the town. She loves to dance, and know the words to most of the songs sung by the band or played by the DJ. She gets her groove on whenever there is an occasion. Whenever there is a party, she fits right in, for music, dance and celebration is an important part of African-American Culture.

6. The Screamer—This woman is psychologically shot. She has yelled so much and so often, that nobody pays her much attention, not even her kids.

7. Sexy Mama-We can't leave sexy mama out for she is also a real part of the culture. She is also known as houchie mama. This sister is flirtatious, revealing, and is often free with her body and sexuality. She took "mini skirts" to a different level. Her motto is the more you show the better. There is a definite freedom in her expression, movements and her style.

Her sexuality is hers and whoever she feels she wants to share it with. She is not shy, nor is she timid.

8. The Sadist-This is the angry Black Female that is mad with the world. She hates the white man and her man, and just about everybody else. She feels that life has served her a bad hand, so she is out for revenge. She fantasizes about what she will say and do to redeem herself. Don't get in her way or she might run you down.

9. Shy Sarah—Sarah is a real "home girl". She is passive, non-assertive, a "don't rock the boat" kind of girl. She is a true marshmallow. Sarah goes along with the program, if there is no program she won't start one. She waits and waits to be rescued by God, a man, a best friend, somebody!

10. (10) Sybil is the one that in some parts of society is viewed as crazy. The book "Sybil" describes her as a woman who had about eight personalities. In African American Culture, Sybil offers the potential to come to terms with various aspects of the personality, for she is every woman. She has harmonized her wild side with her spirituality, her passiveness with her rebellious nature, and the other levels of self. She is comfortable in her own skin, she is at peace, for her heart is open and her mind is free. This woman has been blessed with the realization that she has a choice and right to be whom she wants to be.

SLOWING DOWN

As the Black Woman continues to care for herself, she must be cognizant to slow down, calm down, relax and chill a minute. Rest replenishes our energy, renews our strength and prepares us for what is next. Communication patterns must be addressed. If the Communication style is the "Machine Gun Style" (Dogmatic, harsh, hard, overly verbal, and mean-spirited,) perhaps you can "try a little tenderness." If the communication style is too soft "The Marshmallow Style" (Too Sweet) maybe some assertiveness training is in order. Assertiveness is the middle path that is beyond domination and control. Psychological wholeness lies in a variety of paths or approaches. At the heart of that process is spiritual centering. Spiritual Centering is connected to an ideology, a belief system, and a practice, as it relates to our existence here on this planet. Our spiritual existence transcends time, space, and matter. This is moving to the metaphysical domain _META_=BEYOND, PHYSIC=PHYSICAL. At the heart of this ideology is an abiding faith that whatever has kept the universe in existence for 15 billion years will not fail us now. We might consider drawing on the cosmology of our ancient ancestors that were convinced that there is a higher power in control. This power has provided a level of control to us, to be used by us, to guide and strengthen us. Let us remember that we cannot get lost, for we are safe in the arms of the "One."

"HERMETIC PHILOSOPHY"

10

MENTAL SCIENCE

African spirituality is anchored and steeped in a profound mental science that was passed on from the ancient elders on the continent of Africa. The noticeable expression of African spirituality and its religious manifestations are largely physical, meaning that a great amount of movement, motion, and activity surrounds its expression. Let it not be confusioned that mental forces are not at work. African religious systems are largely based on nature and the intelligence that resides in the natural forces of the earth and its solar systems. African people are people of the sun and some scholars believe that melanin is a conductor of this awesome energy force. Astrology and astronomy tend to be at the heart of most religions. "The wise men follower the Star" The Islamic symbol is a "crescent moon and star." "The Star of David" is the most powerful Jewish symbol. Isn't it interesting that many Christians worship on SUN-DAY? We find Astronomy throughout the religious Diaspora.

Higher knowledge and wisdom is at the heart and soul of African spirituality and its manifestations are in Africa and all over its various global communities. Some scholars hold mental transmutation and alchemy as part and parcel of the ability to tap into and to engage "The Source" or "Divine Energy." This is not child's play, nor is it for the spiritually immature. This is the ability to integrate, assimilate, and demonstrate intelligence. Miracles, healing, and psychic expressions, and the interaction with the spirit world is a super powerful phenomena. All is mind. All is intelligence. (Kybalion)

Ancient Egyptian Thought is based on Hermetic Philosophy. The Kybalion, a source book of this ancient mystical teaching as expressed by Hermes Trismegistus, called "The Great Great" and "Master of Masters. Hermes was an Egyptian Master who was the contemporary of Abraham. Egypt is a birthplace of great mystical teaching and for many "Hidden Wisdom." The Kybalion contains the teachings, spiritual laws and principles that were outlined by Hermes. In it he teaches the spiritual keys that utilize and express this Sacred Mental Science.

Africa has given us much. It is incumbent upon us to learn what and how to best use the gifts that have been bestowed upon us (The Principles). If we can, we are the recipients of the greatest gifts of all. We become self aware, coherent, proficient and masterful. The purpose of this work is to draw from this understanding, and use the rich spiritual and intellectual heritage that is available, and pass it on to others. Understanding these principles and laws can deeply enrich our lives and existence here on this planet.

The Kybalion explores The Seven Hermetic Principles:

I. The Principle of Mentalism
II. The Principle of Correspondence
III. The Principle of Vibration
IV. The Principle of Polarity
V. The Principe of Rhythm
VI. The Principle of Cause and Effect
VII. The Principle of Gender

The Principle of Mentalism

This principle maintains that we live in and are a part of a Mental Universe. Divine mind is the only essential reality. It upholds and is first cause of everything that is, and shall be manifested, or revealed. The "Real World" as we know and don't know it is the expression of "Mind." This "Absolute Power" can be accessed by acknowledgement of this divine power in the universe and understanding the spiritual law from which it operates. The ancient Egyptians called this power "The All."

Mentalism is expressed in creation, creativity, and productivity. It can be called forth through faith, meditation, study, practice, and motion. The word is another building block in the evolution of mentalism. The word becomes life and has its own correspondence. By using the "right" words we attract the experiences we want.

African Americans and others from the Diaspora are "Word People." This is one major way in which they express, verbally. This is also a way that divine Mind expresses itself from the vibration of words and the meaning they represent. Coming from an "Oral Tradition" the use of this principle was a natural way of tapping into this awesome force. Connecting with "G-d Mind"(Mentalism) is a part of early conditioning and programming that set the stage for the survival and success of African Americans, and their continued deeply spiritual essence.

The Principle of Correspondence

"As above, so below, so above" The Kybalion

The Principle of Correspondence holds that there are many planes and dimension of mind and existence. The use of this principle is amplified by understanding the first principle Mentalism, whereby we understand first that we exist in a mental, organized, and intelligent universe that is lawful and orderly.

This principle or law of correspondence suggests that we can put into place or into operation a universe of our making by mixing and matching dimensions by mental imaging, rituals, knowledge and developing a verbal and mental picture of the world in which we desire. We can call this "reality" into being by knowing that there are higher and deeper dimensions. We create and interact with them by uniting those worlds through the power of imagination by seeing and looking between the cracks and under the veil to glimpse the whole, the sacred," the ALL."

African peoples are highly evolved creative and spiritual beings. A strong a powerful mind facilitated this ability to be multidimensional. Physical strength is equivalent to mental strength. The root of this correspondence is strength. Again, the mind tells the body what to do and vice versa. The early ancestors were able to connect dimensions and worlds by treating them as one. In African Cosmology the ancestors were not "Dead" just operating on a different dimension of time and space and existence. The relationship was not over after death, often the relationship was intensified. (Deepen)

African Americans are quick to tell you "That's Deep." They look for the profound, the provocative, the unusual; it is apart of their cosmology and belief system. By the innate understanding of the principle of Correspondence, they were able to transform a one dimensional existence into a multilayered and highly spiritual one.

The Principle of Vibration

Nothing is stagnating; all things move, change, vibrate. The level of vibration is not always constant, however. Human beings can raise or lower their vibration based on what they say, think, believe, and do. With an understanding of the fact that everything is in motion, everything is energy, one can then began to connect the dots to spiritual realization.

African people operate on the bases of vibration. African-Americans will comment after a religious service "The Spirit was high" or the anointing was present. After a Party, "That party was hot" and after meeting a person, African-Americans may comment, "I got a good vibe or I got a bad vibe about that person." This is standard conversation in African-American Communities." This is interacting with energy, and assessing its impact. These interactions are deeply vibrational and utilize this principle.

African people are often highly energetic, active, moving, and physical. They use these abilities as ways to gauge and interact with varying vibration levels. Many have become masterful in this endeavor and the use of these abilities to serve as a conduit for psychic and physical power

This calls our attention to the question: Does this universe operate on principles and laws, or does it not?

Principle of Polarity

The Principle of Polarity holds that the apparent contradictions, differences, and opposites we experience are simple figments of our imagination. That duality only exists in our minds and not in reality. There is no separation, no paradox; everything is one. Heat and cold, good and bad, light and dark are only degrees of the same thing. We are able to fuse the differences by this understanding and by becoming proficient at making adjustments in the vibrations or in the alteration of the inner thermostatic conditions.

Chaos theory tells us that seeming contradictions gives us the opportunity to create new forms of equilibrium and relationships, therefore, allowing for transformation and harmony. Understanding and using this principle can serve as a great tool for internal and external peace. "We are one." The Jamaican creed is 'Out of Many, One.' This creed has universal application.

African-Americans have drawn on this principle in our everyday lives. A major example of this is the African American Mantra "ITS ALL GOOD." This expression has caused this people to examine and re-evaluate daily situations and scenarios. Viewing life within this context allows one to tap into the Principle of Polarity.

The Principle of Rhythm

Rhythm is motion that is ordered and measured. The Principle of Rhythm reminds us that the universe operates on rhythm and on order. The rising and the setting of the sun. The change of the seasons; winter, spring, summer, and fall. The high and low tides. From this principle you draw inference that one may counter the effects of low times with the realization that with timing, pacing and waiting equilibrium will be restored. The Cycle will once again turn in your favor. With this understanding one learns not to work against oneself but with oneself and the universe. This comes largely from paying attention to life, and by paying attention to nature. The universe has its rhythm, and so do we all.

African people are masters of rhythm. The drumming, music and dance are just a few examples of how this principle is demonstrated externally. From this principle one can gain a sense of security. African-Americans are known to tell you that "Everything will be alright." In time everything will. African' Americans interpret this principle with a familiar slogan; "GO WITH THE FLOW".

The Principle of Cause and Effect

Everything happens according to divine law. Whatever you plant will grow, whatever you reap you sow. If you put something into life you get an equal or better return. This principle requires like all others, your participation and the understanding of the law. The principle of causation holds that our thoughts, words and actions set a form in motion. "What comes around, Goes around." This is another Mantra of African American thought that is common in the culture.

A favorable outcome follows a favorable input. Many African Americas are regular churchgoers, givers and hard workers in their religious institutions. It is believed that they are "blessed" by their endeavors because they embrace this principle of cause and effect or reaping and sowing. In their spiritual disciplines this was also the case; serve, pray, fast, worship. The end result will be a high level of spiritual mastery. If you put something into it, you will get something out. This is simplistic, but at the same time profound and extremely beneficial in building a consciousness for success and spiritual power. Enslaved Africans and those who paid the high price for liberation must have started and continued with this end in mind.

The Principle of Gender

This principle holds that Gender exists on all planes and transcends sexual differences on a physical level. Masculine and feminine energy brings forth birth on all levels of existence material, intellectual as well as on the spiritual level. No creation is possible without the interaction of masculine and feminine energy. The logic and intuition must harmonize, so must physical and spiritual. This theory embraces a balance in the masculine and the feminine energies before true progress is made.

This principle teaches to value, affirm and value both contribution inputs, and works with both types of forces for the perfection of an idea or practice.

Male and female presence is clearly seen and valued in African-American life. Perhaps this is one of the reasons that the Woman's Movement never took on the same form in the Black Community as it did in the Anglo Community. Women are highly valued in the African and African American life. The priests, the mid wives, the healers the mothers. were all highly valued in the community. This recognition is a part of the African and African American belief system that the feminine and the masculine forces must work together and be harmonized in order to make for a complete and workable solution, for the needs of the individual and community.

Conclusion

The purpose of this analysis is to assert and identify some of the spiritual principles that have allowed the African American population to be strong and to assert themselves physically, mentally and spiritually. Additionally, it seeks to draw attention to the fact that mental science is very much apart of African culture and its retentions. The utilizations of these principles helped to make for a community that is viable and persistent.

It is hoped that African People will view themselves within a context of mental and spiritual greatness by understanding the genealogy of their people and their sciences. Along with the understanding that these powerful laws were given to African ancestors ages ago. Obviously they were ready and able to receive this information, and again at the center of intellectual and spiritual thought. It is hoped that revisiting this information will assist in bringing back the knowledge and respectability of a group of people who were too long denied their rightful place at the religious and intellectual tables of humanity.

African and African American input is essential to the development of a strong and viable spiritual and human community, whereby all can gain access to a wealth of information that would assist in the understanding of the truth: The truth is we are not only Human Beings but Spiritual Beings.

"A MOTHER'S DREAM DEFERRED"

11

AFRICAN AMERICAN WOMEN & EVANGELISM

The Black woman has played a major role in the promoting, utilizing and passing on from one generation to the next African American spiritual practices. It has been said, "There would be no Black Church without the Black Women. As the old African Proverb well states:" The Women hold up half of the sky ..."

Sojourner Truth was one of the greatest evangelists of the mid 19th century. Born Isabella Baumfree, in Ulster County, New York in 1797, she was sold on many occasions and suffered greatly under the hardships of slavery, but her mother had a deep and unwavering Christian faith that helped to sustain her throughout her life. Truth was the first Pentecostal out of the Great Awakening Movement of the 1840's. She saw visions. That was how is she came about the name Sojourner Truth. Also, Harriett Tubman, the great Abolitionist, and remembered for her work with the "Underground Railroad, had an AME Zion Church in Auburn, New York. She too was a minister of the gospel, and who saw, and spoke with "God."

There has been debate (the debate continues) and controversy over the years, as it relates to Women and Ministry. At one point in time, many Black churches were adamant in their position that women should not be pastors or ministers. As a result, her role as minister and leader took another shape and form and as a result the Black woman became the ministers during prayer and bible study, generally in their own homes, called "Houses of Prayer." Others who were able to provide ministry in the churches were called missionaries and evangelists, rarely pastors and preachers. These trends are still active in many Black churches today. Here we see the notion of the woman as both adored and scorned. Women tend to be more dedicated to the church, yet this paradox exists.

At various points in History, women spiritualists have met with resistance. The Noted "Witch Hunts" in the United States and in other parts of the world is a real life phenomenon which targeted men and women. Many "Religious People" could not accept nor handle the sacred and awesome power that women have. As a result, to silence them, they were demonized, burned and victimized by other forms of murder and called witches or winches. Perhaps they were also viewed as a threat to the males' spiritual dominance because of her relationship with the divine.

A stark example of an attempt to suppress women can be seen in the early twentieth century of the Black Pentecostal movement at that time, women were not even allowed to sit in the pulpit. This is true even though in the psychological literature women have more paranormal (psychic) dreams than men by two to one. It was also noted when I made a recent trip to Salvador, Brazil, that it is the women that provide leadership at the Candomble Houses, which are African Based Religious Centers The deeply spiritual nature of women cannot be denied, and it was not denied, in terms of the spread of Africanized Christianity in the United States. And so, I recall my mother:

Zenovious Sermons Stripling (1919–1999)

The date of this writing is May 8, 2005 (Mother's Day). It was deemed fitting on this day to remember my mother and her methods, practices, and service as it relates to African American Women and Evangelism. In so doing she becomes a living memorial and I pay homage and respect to the ancestors and make her in the history of African American Spirituality accessible to the living.

Zenovious Sermons Stripling's role as teacher/missionary/evangelist was a position of great importance to her. This "Divine Appointment" and her commitment and proficiency in it, made her "Great" to the people within her sphere of contact. As I reflect on her life, I think of so many spiritually gifted women and men that I have experienced over the years. Many are forgotten by most, and few even remember their names, and most importantly, their contributions to the advancement of knowledge, culture, and the scared sciences.

This documentation is important for it gives them a place in history, and provides others the opportunity to understand the historical and spiritual evolution of a people. Additionally, a purpose of this work is to provide some of the keys, or certainly links to the manifestation of advancing knowledge and power in our lives. In this light, we have tools to unlock the door to the metaphysical domain. As a result, future generations will understand what allowed our ancestors to survive and thrive during difficult periods of history in this country.

When Zenovious Sermons Stripling spoke people listened. She was very unorthodox in her methodology. Dramatic, practical, totally engaging, no non-sense, assertive, serious, and not shy in the least. Many during her era, from around the 1950's to 1980's would say she had "Holy Boldness" that mixed and mingled with what is called the "Anointing" (Intensified Spiritual Energy). When observing one of her sessions, you knew you were in the presence of an undeniable, inescapable presence that gave witness to the highest power and force in the universe. Many of her attributes are difficult to put into words, but I must try.

Each generation has it geniuses. The genius in us is the activation of the higher self. Zenovious Stripling could tap into her genius and it could be expressed in the "Spoken Word." Not just words, but spiritually charges and potent words. Her words went forth with electricity and magnetism that searched out the innermost corners of a persons being and found residence.

Her sermons were rich with symbolism and straight forward language that was titillating, passionate, stimulating and exciting. African Spirituality is just that, IT IS EXCITEMENT. Her word selections were piercing and stunning and contained so much energy that many would go into trance or spiritual possession just listening and receiving her words. It was as if her words became alive and entered us.

She was a spiritual scientist of sort, a metaphysician of the highest order, a magnificent artist that had the ability to paint you a picture of your life with God and your life without God. She meticulously and methodologically took you on a spiritual journey through the portals of "Heaven and Hell" and brought you back by sheer will, unharmed but in search and longing for a "Better Life" Her ministry as a Missionary/Evangelist caused a transformation within the individual. She used her voice, her tones, her penetrating eyes, and body movements. "Holistic Engagement" would be the term to most adequately describe her methodology. I watched her intently as a child and as an adult decided that I wanted some of that "Anointing".

As I reflect on some of the characteristics, habits and behaviors that made my mother great. I would summarize them as follows:

1. She was a firm believer in the existence of an all powerful supernatural force (God)
And believed that this power was accessible to human beings (THE POWER OF FAITH)

2. Her work was activated by an awesome love for God and for her fellow sisters and brothers. (THE POWER OF LOVE)

3. She had an incredible memory, i.e. events, scriptures, ideas, concepts and other facts That would allow one to make connections and draw parallels that would make her positions clear and sound. (THE POWER OF CONNECTIVITY)

4. She had a deep knowledge and understanding of the human condition. (THE POWER OF KNOWLEDGE)

5. She could disrobe and disarm a person by her logic and conviction leaving one open to a spiritual transformation. (THE POWER OF TRANSFORMATION)

6. She was an excellent storyteller who could bring a story to life. Having an interesting beginning that builds to a crescendo and further to a spiritual explosion. (THE POWER OF THE WORD)

During and after her sermons people were MOVED: Some cried profusely and became overwhelmed with emotions, some screamed as a release, and others were consumed temporarily by a non—human entity or energy, termed the 'Holy Ghost' in the Pentecostal experience.

African/African Americans in the United States and in the Diaspora as part and parcel of our cosmology have embraced and experienced this "Ghost-Like" Entity that could inhabit and consume a person's mind, behavior, thoughts, and body for transformative purposes.

When my mother gave her "Messages" (like so many other black ministers) she became transfixed, (someone/something else in addition to her persona) that gave her power and knowledge beyond compare. This force was able to channel through her wisdom, spiritual truths and abilities that far exceeded her eleventh grade formal education. Her wisdom could be as profound as scholars and academics, along with her delivery style and ability to engage the hearts and minds of others. To summarize these phenomena, I recall one of her favorite songs:

"This joy that I have the world didn't give it to me, this joy that I have the world didn't give it to me, the world didn't give it and the world can't take it away."

"This knowledge that I have the world didn't give it to me; this knowledge that I have the world didn't give it to me. This knowledge that I have the world didn't give it to me, the world didn't give it and the world can't take it away."

An important question for me is: How did she obtain this power? She started everyday with a song and prayer early in the mornings, while still in bed, in the bathroom, cooking in the kitchen, driving us to school, waiting in the bank, or grocery store, working in the yard, she was constant with a song and prayer. Sometimes a prayer would lead into a song; sometimes a song would lead to a prayer. Sometimes she would combine the song and the prayer. At times, it would be a soft humming, other times they were loud and full blown. This depended on where we were at the time and "THE STATE OF THE EMERGENCY" OR NEED.

The greatest gift my mother gave me was her example and her methodology for awakening the spiritual energy that lie within me and within us all. However, in many cases it remains dormant. I have chosen to use her practices at times in my own life, and I have found them very effective, along with new models of spiritual transformation I have obtained.

Again her methods were based on consistency and focus attention. Her meditative directives along with a strong belief system activated the "God Presence" in her life. These formula that I described is what I believe was central to her profound power as a minister. This, along with her choice to say "yes" to spirit and "yes" to her gift were part of the spiritual recipe for greatness. Saying "yes" immediately brings to mind another of her songs:

> "I say yes Lord yes, to your will and to your way, I say yes lord yes, I will trust you and obey. When your spirit speak to me with my whole heart I agree, and my answer will be yes Lord, Yes."

These attitudes, behaviors and expressions of gratitude, submission, steadfastness, and receptivity were foundational and highly anchoring in great evangelist's ministries. My mother provides one example. I ask myself often do these gifts run in families. I think so either through nature or nurture or perhaps a combination of the two. It can be passed on by the socialization or enculturation process or maybe it is coded in the genes by the genetic memory of our ancestors. This is a mystery that I don't fully understand.

My mother would say "it was predestined before the foundation of the earth" its God's will." SO BE IT. (ASHE) (AMEN)

THANKS MOM! IT IS FINISHED!

"THE BLACK SOUL LIVES …"

CONCLUSION

The purpose of this book is to provide a glimpse into African American thought and life, by discussing some of the factors that have formulated and shaped this group of people. This framework is by no means an exhaustive formulation, for Black Culture is highly extensive, multidimensional and ever changing and evolving. There are however, some common threads and similar themes that inform Black Culture. Further reflection and interrogation of the culture and its diaspora is needed to develop the framework necessary to better understand African American People, and to put their lives and culture in its proper perspective. This is indeed an ongoing and continuous process.

This manuscript is about remembering and recording some of the aspects and stories of Black Life here in the United States largely from an insider's perspective. There are others pieces to this vast, complex and rich cultural dialog yet to be to discussed and written about. This is a work in progress both personally and collectively, because "the half has not been told". Let us commit and recommit ourselves to tell our stories and our truths so that "*The Souls of Black Folks*" (and other folk) are honored, remembered, and carried with us on our journey through this life. We need this knowledge for continuity, perspective and wholeness. Additionally, we must continue the work, because there is a cultural heritage we must bequeath our children and those yet unborn. They need to know that their fore parents did not come to this country as an empty slate, but with thousands of years of stored up energy, thereby they were able to withstand and transcend the harshness of slavery, "Jim Crow" Laws, and ongoing discrimination. They need to know that those Ancestors stolen off the continent of Africa were highly skilled workers and were able to do things in many cases that the captors could not do, such as the planting and cultivating rice and other crops, building houses, railroads, and even the furniture for the plantation owners' homes. They need to know how to tap into the spiritual power that has helped to make Black people strong, wise, and creative. They need to know that much wrong has been done to our people, both to our psyches and bodies yet, we are still here, and helped to build this country and its economy. Additionally, African

People have shared their fun and fascinating culture with this country and the world. For American (US) Culture is largely Black Culture. Again, let us recount the lives and experiences of the Ancestors on whose shoulders we now stand. As a result we will stand tall; we will stand high, and regain our rightful place in the cosmos.

REFERENCES

Asante, M. *Afrocentricity.* Trenton, New Jersey: African New World Press, 1991.

Athey, L. *Latin America.* New Jersey: Globe/Modern Curriculum Press, 1987.

Atwater, E. and Duffy, K. *The Psychology of Living*, 7th Edition. Upper Saddle River, New Jersey: Prentice Hall, 2002.

Bass, T. "Traditional African Psychotherapy: An Interview with Thomas Adeoye Lambo." Reprinted from Reinventing the Future. Reading, MA Addison Wesley. 1994.

Blaze, C. and Blaze, G. *Power Prayer*. Avon, MA: Adams Media, 2004.

Berry, M.F. and Blassingame. *Long Memory: The Black Experience in America.* New York: Oxford University Press, 1983.

Carter, J. "African Religion." *Religion & Culture.* Ed. R. Scupin. New Jersey: Prentice Hall, 2000.

Courlander, H. *Haiti Singing.* Chapel Hill: University of North Carolina Press, 1939.

Crahan, M.C. and F.W. Knight, Eds. *Africa and the Caribbean: The Legacies of a Link.* Maryland: John Hopkins University Press, 1979.

Cunard, N. *Negro an Anthology*. New York: Continuum Press, 1996.

Du Bois, W.E.B. *The Souls of Black Folk*. New York: Bantam Books. 1963.

Dunham, K. *Dances of Haiti.* University of California, Los Angeles: Center for Afro American Studies, 1983.

Ember & Ember. *Anthropology.* 8th edition. New Jersey: Prentice Hall, 1996.

Evans. M. Mind Body Spirit: *A Practical Guide to Natural Therapies of Health and Well Being.* New York: Anness Publishing. 2000.

Feltman, J. Editor. *The Prevention How-To Dictionary of Healing* Remedies and Techniques. Emmaus, Pennsylvania: Rodale Press. 1992.

Fillmore, C. *The Revealing Word: A Dictionary of Metaphysical Terms*. Unity Village, Missouri: Unity Books, 1997.

Finn, Julio. *The Bluesman: The Musical Heritage of Black Men and Women in the Americas*. New York: Interlink Books, 1991.

Fontana, D. *The Secret Language of Dreams*. San Francisco: Chronicle Books, 1994.

Frazier, E.F. *The Negro Church in America*. New York: Schocken Books, 1963.

Freke, T. and Gandy, P. *The Complete Guide to World Mysticism.* London: Piatkus Books, 1997.

Glazer, N. and D.P. Miynihan. *Beyond the Melting Pot.* 2nd edition. Cambridge, Massachusetts: MIP Press, 1970.

Herskovits, M.J. *Myth of the Negro Past*. Boston: Beacon Press, 1958.

Harner, M. *The Way of the Shaman*. New York: Harper Collins, 1990.

Holloway, Joseph E. *Africanisms in American Culture*. Bloomington, Indianapolis: Indiana Press, 1990.

Hunter, D. *The Lyric Poet: A Blues Continuum*. Brooklyn, New York: Caribbean Diaspora Press, 2001.

Hurston, Z.N. "The Sanctified Church." *The Folklore Writings of Zora Neale Hurston*. Berkeley, CA: Turtle Island Foundation, 1981.

Keesing, F. M. *Cultural Anthropology*. New York: Holt, Rinehart and Winston, 1965.

Kilson, M.L. and R.I. Rotberg. "The African Diaspora Interpretive Essays." *Religions of the Caribbean*. Ed. George Eaton Simpson. Cambridge: Harvard University, 1976.

Kinney, Esi Sylvia. "Africanisms in Music and Dance in the Americas." *Black Life and Culture in the United States.* Ed. Rhonda Goldstein. New York: Thomas Y. Crowell Company, Inc., 1971.

Kornblum, W. *Sociology in a Changing World.* Florida: Holt, Rinehart and Winston Inc., 1991.

Levin, L.W. *Black Culture and Black Consciousness.* New York: Oxford University Press, 1977.

M' Bow, B. "*Sacred Vision She Who Possesses the Sacred Eye*" Article Published in *The Decent of the Lwa. Journey through Haitian Mythology the Works of Hersa Barjon.* Broward County Library and Kosanba Santa Barbara. December 2004.

Neimark, P. *The Way of the Orisa.* New York: Harper Collins Publishers. 1993.

Parrillo, V.N. *Strangers to these Shores: Race and Ethnic Relations in the United States.* Macmillan Publishing Company, 1990.

Richards, D.M. *Let the Circle Be Unbroken.* New Jersey: The Red Sea Press, 1980.

Three Initiates. *The Kybalion: Hermetic Philosophy.* Chicago, ILL. The Yogi Publishing Society Masonic Temple, 1912.

Thornton, J. *Africa and Africans in the Making of the Atlantic World 1400-1800.* London: Cambridge University Press, 1998.

Stostak, M. *Nisa: The Life and Words of a Kung Woman.* Massachusetts: Harvard University Press, 1981.

Van De Castle, R. *Our Dreaming Mind.* New York: Ballantine Books, 1994.

Yves-Leloup, J. *The Gospel of Mary Magdalene.* Rochester: Inner Traditions International, 2002

Baker, Phyllis." Interview with the Reverend Dr. Mary Tumpkin, "Universal Truth Center," Miami Gardens, Florida, June 2005.

RECORD YOUR PRAYERS, MUSIC, & DREAMS HERE FOR THE NEXT SEVEN DAYS

978-0-595-44231-7
0-595-44231-5

Made in the USA
Lexington, KY
21 March 2010